ON REFLECTION SERIES

LIMPING
towards the
SUNRISE

SERMONS IN SEASON

Richard Holloway

Series Editor: Duncan B Forrester

SAINT ANDREW PRESS
EDINBURGH

*The Publisher acknowledges
financial assistance from
The Drummond Trust
towards the publication of this volume.*

First published in 1996 by
SAINT ANDREW PRESS
121 George Street, Edinburgh EH2 4YN

ISBN 0 7152 0711 3

British Library Cataloguing in Publication Data
A catalogue record for this book
is available from the British Library.

ISBN 0715207113

Cover design concept by Mark Blackadder.
Cover photograph by Paul Turner.
Printed by BPC-AUP Aberdeen Ltd.

Contents

Series Editor's Introduction

ALL down the ages Christians have reflected on their faith and its bearing on life. These reflections have taken a great variety of forms, but one of the most common has been the sermon. For generations notable preachers were well-known public figures, and books of sermons were a well-known literary genre. In many places people queued to hear great preachers, whose sermons were reported in the press, and discussed and dissected afterwards. Sermons launched great movements of mission, and revival, and social change. Sometimes influential preachers were imprisoned by the authorities so that their disturbing challenge should not be heard.

Nowhere was this tradition more lively than in Scotland. But today, some people say, the glory has departed. If you want to find great preaching today, the critics say, go to Africa, or Latin America, or to Black churches in the States. No longer in Scotland do people pack in their hundreds into huge churches to hear great preachers. The sermon seems to have lost its centrality in Scottish life. The conviction and the emotional surcharge that once sustained a great succession of notable preachers seems hard to find today. Has secularisation destroyed the appetite for sermons? Has the modern questioning of authority eroded the preaching office? Do Christians no longer reflect on their faith, or do they do it in other and newer ways?

This series of books shows that the tradition of preaching is still very much alive and well. It has changed, it is true, and it has adapted to new circumstances and new challenges. It is not the same as it was in the long afterglow of the Victorian pulpit. Reflection by the Scots on their faith, as these books illustrate, is perhaps more varied than it was in the past, and their sermons are briefer. But Scottish preaching is still passionate, thoughtful, biblical, challenging, and deeply concerned with the relevance of the gospel to the needs of today's world.

The reflections on the Christian faith in these books are challenging, disturbing, nourishing. They proclaim a Word that is alive and active, and penetrates to the depths of things, a Word that speaks of hope and worth, of forgiveness and new beginnings, of justice, peace and love. And so they invite the reader to engage afresh with the everlasting gospel.

Duncan B Forrester
EDINBURGH

ON REFLECTION ...

Other titles available in this series

Wrestle and Fight and Pray
John L Bell

Laughter and Tears
James A Whyte

A Workable Belief
Gilleasbuig Macmillan

Go by the Book
Robert Davidson

For
Neil
and
Marily Macvicar

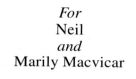

Preface

A FRIEND recently accused me of 'leaving no thought unpublished'. I am therefore sensitive about this book of sermons and almost feel the need to offer an explanation for it. Duncan Forrester kindly invited me two years ago to contribute to a series of Scottish Preachers he was editing for Saint Andrew Press, and I agreed. This book, however, is more a book of preaching than a book of sermons. The sermons themselves come in the middle, sandwiched between a homiletical essay and an epilogue on the practice of preaching. I had originally planned to place this section on the preacher's vocation at the beginning, but Duncan has persuaded me that it is better at the end, where it can be read by students and ministers and, if they choose, ignored by everyone else.

The sermons themselves are published as delivered, with their local references intact. On reading them over I have noticed how non-inclusive the language is in sermons preached some time ago. That, too, I have left uncorrected, though I would pay more attention to the matter in sermons preached today. I am grateful to Duncan for suggesting the book, and to my secretary Christine Roy, as always, for her contribution in putting it together from an untidy file of sermons.

Richard Holloway
EDINBURGH

Limping
towards the Sunrise

I ALWAYS take a hike on Hogmanay, with a few friends. We do a loop in the Pentlands, walking in at Bavelaw, climbing West Kip, East Kip and Scald Law, and coming back to Bavelaw via the Green Cleugh. The hike was inaugurated in 1975 on December 31st, just before a friend went back to Africa. We toasted his health each year in the same sheep pen, during the lunch break of left-over turkey and good claret. The tradition was interrupted when I was in the USA in the eighties. When I returned to Edinburgh in 1986, I started it up again.

David joined us the first year I was back and I think I know now why he never joined us again. He was an experienced walker, a systematic Munro-bagger, who kept detailed diaries of all his walks. He was probably the most experienced walker of the group that joined me that Hogmanay in 1986. We all knew he was quiet, a contemplative sort of man, but we hadn't realised how slow he was. After the two miles walk in, he was about half a mile behind us; and by the time we were on the top of West Kip he was a slowly moving dot on the horizon. (It was not until after his death that I found out he had stayed back to accompany a slow walker who was wearing borrowed boots.) Unperturbed, he caught up with us as we were toasting absent friends. He smiled quietly at our noisy exuberance as he ate his sandwich. On the final leg through Green Cleugh and back to the cars at Red Moss he stayed with us, though it is probably just as true to say we stayed with him, as we slithered through the muddy snow.

Back at the house we left our boots on newspapers in the hall and warmed ourselves with mulled wine and hot pies. David was a kind presence in the midst of the banter, his eyes gentle and observant. But he never took part again in one of these noisy jaunts at the year's end and I often wondered why. I continued to hear about his walking. I knew that he'd bagged his last Munro and was now lifting his eyes to the hills of Ireland. That's where he died. His walking style was miles removed from mine, but we both liked long, solitary expeditions.

On Easter Monday 1990 he took off for a week's walking in Ireland. People had spoken about the remarkable quality of the addresses he'd delivered at the Three Hours on Good Friday and even someone as modest as David must have known that he had touched many hearts. The week of walking ended on Mount Galtymore in Tipperary. The sun was warm on his back as he came down off the hill and he decided to find a place to sit down and fill in his diary. Just before the track that led out on to the road, he found a gentle grassy slope that looked down the valley. He sat there, filling his eyes with the scene and took out the diary. He'd phoned Helen the night before and sent everyone postcards. It had been a perfect week's walking, in spite of the Irish weather, but today was lovely and he would record his thanks. 'Low Sunday,' he wrote, 'Sunday 22 April 1990', and then his heart stopped, he slipped over onto his side, as if asleep, very peaceful, with the diary open by his hand, his journey ended.

Next morning, sitting round the table in the little parlour at the Rectory, stunned by her father's death on an Irish hillside, reminiscing about him through her tears, Janet wondered what it was about the clergy that made so many of them such dedicated walkers. For some reason I diverted the conversation onto another clerical obsession (one I *don't* share) – railways – but Janet's question stayed with me and I got the answer the following night. Bruce Chatwin was almost certainly the most heroic walker of our century and he expounds his doctrine of walking in his book *Songlines,* but it was from something else he wrote that I got the clue. Chatwin died in January 1989 and a posthumous collection of pieces he wrote was published called *What Am I Doing Here.* In a piece about Werner Herzog, the German film director, he writes this:

He was the only person with whom I could have a one-to-one conversation on what I would call the sacramental aspect of walking. He and I share a belief that walking is not simply thera-peutic for one's self but is a poetic activity that can cure the world of its ills. In 1974, when he heard Lotte Eisner was dying, he set out walking through ice and snow, from Munich to Paris, confident that somehow he could walk away her sickness. By the time he reached her apartment she had recovered and went on to live another ten years.[1]

Walking is prayer and sacrament and it helps to heal the world. As sacrament, it is the outward and visible sign of our transience, our wayfarer status. Life is something we are passing through; it's a journey we are on. Chatwin loved nomads and the purity of their values. He believed that most of the ills we suffer from are the result of settling down, not moving on; of trying to own and possess and exploit creation, instead of moving through it gently, wondering at it as we travel, seeking only an eternal city. David had understood that doctrine and lived by it. He had the simplicity, the unclutteredness of the true nomad. There was nothing possessive or acquisitive about him. I suspect that much of that was natural to him, but some of it was learned during 16 formative years in India. When he came back to Edinburgh in 1983, he brought with him something of the depth and stillness of Holy India, the sense that we are strangers and exiles on earth, homesick for God, but, nevertheless, greatly enjoying the journey home. Walking as sacrament, then: no better word could describe David's love for walking, with all the lore and liturgy of it: boots and gaiters, map and compass, and a good Gortex robe.

But walking is also praying. Solitary walking is both contem-plative prayer and intercession. I'm not a contemplative walker, something in me always wants to push on too fast, but I intercede as I walk. David did both. Like the best prayers, David never hurried.

He moved over the hills at a contemplative pace, seeing deeply, taking it all into himself. But walking is most profoundly a kind of intercession, because the solitary walker's mind is filled with images and faces from his own life, scraps of memory, regrets, remembered joys, loved ones. You touch them all with love and remembrance as you move on, watching the film playing in your head. Walking releases the switch of memory and plays back to you the movie of your life.

And walking is also metaphor and judgement. As a man walks, so does he live, or so I have discovered about myself. That discovery is a gift David sent back to me. I have always been a compulsively fast walker, intent on covering the territory, not on looking round me as I move on. This strange need to push on, to eat up the miles, has spoiled several long walks I have done. I have turned them into endurance tests. Of course, endurance is an inescapable aspect of long distance walking, but is it the reason we do it? In David's case I am sure it wasn't. He was a contemplative walker, a true walker. Walking should be intrinsically meditational, slow enough to permit observation, fast enough to help the mind disengage. In classic prayer there are various techniques for disengaging the mind from its obsessions, such as beads and mantras. The idea is to find a mechanism that concentrates the attention by intentionally distracting it, thereby releasing the unconscious, freeing the heart to do its thing. I have found that running helps me to do this; so does intense walking. Difficulties have been resolved, themes discovered, as I have powered my way over a hill or round a jogging track. But the distances travelled have all been metaphorical or figurative. They have all been journeys round my own mind and I am grateful that I have learned to use my body to stimulate and direct my mind. Even so, it is all solitary, not to say solipsistic. I have gone out onto the hills to get into myself, not to get in touch with them. I could tell you what went on in my own mind, rarely what went on outside me. I'm not very good at map reading. I can't quite line up the map with what I see around me, except in the most general way. I'm not even very good at figuring out what direction I'm going in and have often doubted the very compass I've been carrying. The combination of passion for solitary walking and directional incompetence has often got me seriously lost, though I have invariably muddled my way back onto the trail.

If I were more in touch with my surroundings they might be more in touch with me, instead of presenting themselves to me as baffled natives before a monoglot tourist. In fact, a tourist is what I increasingly feel like. Tourists are not travellers. They carry their culture and all their assumptions with them. They move through the countries they visit as though they were seeing them on TV in their own dens back home. Travellers are different; they journey to meet the other, to make contact, not with themselves but with what lies beyond themselves. Tourists pass through, travellers go into the strange land. And the pace is important. If walking is a way of getting from X to Y, and Y is where you want to be, then speed is what counts, covering the territory is the aim. But if walking is a way of getting in touch, a sort of communion, then the pace has to be fast enough to be serious, but slow enough for observation. David had it about right. His diaries noticed things, mine simply measured the distance.

A log I kept of a recent walk along the South Downs Way illustrates the problem:

Nothing particularly philosophical or reflective to say, except that I did my old trick of simply covering the territory. There are contemplative walkers, walkers who look at everything, notice what they're doing. I tend to be someone who just wants to cover the distance and what I think I wanted from this particular long hike was an endurance test. I wanted to put myself through my paces again and see whether I could still do it, and I suppose I can answer Yes – just. By the end of the week I should be in much better shape than I am at the moment, but having done twenty miles today, the verdict has to be not too bad. I suppose there's something to be said for my philosophy of hiking. I find the actual movement, the covering of territory itself quite liberating. The mind ranges but I wasn't doing any systematic thinking. I was essentially covering the miles, pushing on, suppressing fantasies of long, cool drinks and lovely pub lunches. Tomorrow I'll probably push on less neurotically but I'll try to do another twenty miles. I'm not sure where I'll spend the night.

On the following day I was still in the grip of the same compulsion. I was walking through some of the loveliest countryside in England, but my log reflects the distance covered, the act of passing through, not the places traversed. I was aware of the Downs around me and the English Channel miles to the south, but my principal memory is of the chalky track beneath my feet and my desire to eat up the miles. The log for the next day reflects this dreary fixation:

I've walked over twenty-two miles today and my legs tell me I'm overdoing it. I've been meditating on why I have this compulsion simply to cover territory. As I said in yesterday's note, I treat these walks as endurance tests. I don't spend enough time looking at the beauty around me, although I do spend some time on that. I seem compelled to cover the mileage and pit myself against my own tiredness. It's a weird thing and I'm not entirely sure what it's about. Jeannie says I'm half mad. Anyway, I've decided to keep the Sabbath here tomorrow, rest up and hope that some of the tiredness will go away and set out on Monday for the second half. I've covered over forty miles in two days. On Monday I'll probably aim to do another twenty. At this rate I'll be at the Hampshire border by Tuesday night, which is where I'm thinking of stopping, since that's strictly speaking where the South Downs Way ends.

I managed to turn the throttle down when I resumed the walk on the Monday and took three enjoyable days to cover the forty miles to the Hampshire border at Buriton, which I reached in the early afternoon on Wednesday. I walked into Petersfield and was on a train to Waterloo by 4.45.

It was on the fourth day of walking that I remembered David on the Hogmanay Hike in 1986. I had an easy twelve mile hike from

Amberley to Cocking. It was my wounds that slowed me down. I had developed some heroic blisters on the second day, which I'd treated with the new stuff that covers them with a skin-like substance. 'I bet David never got a blister in his life,' I thought, as I limped up Bignor Hill. I remembered his meticulous preparations, his attention to his equipment and the unhurried way he walked. It was all in mysterious contrast to my own slapdash and impulsive style. What am I hurrying for?

I remembered the Chairman of the Board of Governors of Winsor School in Boston. At prize-giving day each year he made exactly the same short speech in which he exhorted the girls in their walk through life to take time to smell the flowers. David smelled them and probably knew them all by name. The journey was important for him, not just the journey's end. Chatwin had the same outlook. The journey is its own end, its own meaning. If we fail to grasp that, we fail to grasp the paradox of time. De Caussade, the French Catholic priest and spiritual writer, called it the Sacrament of the Present Moment. We are only ever in the present moment, only there can we live. Those of us who live prospectively, looking only to the journey's end and not to the journey itself, cannot be said to be truly living in real time at all, we're always rushing up the down escalator.

I think now that David sensed that about our Hogmanay hikes. Their Zen wasn't right for him. It was very Western Male, dominant, assertive, unresponsive. It was commodity walking, walking as consumption not communion. In fact, it was a parable of the human condition at the tail end of the millennium. We have been using the creation to exercise our own compulsions, treating it as a means not an end. I don't know where this comes from, or even how culpable we are for it, but it seems wise to try to moderate it, to slow down and look around. This is going to be difficult for me, but if I can't slow down by an act of mind itself, maybe my sore feet will do it for me. You can't race ahead when you are limping.

Even so, I don't want to fall into the boring trap of total self-condemnation. Being the way I am must mean something, have some kind of value. It occurs to me that I am more like Jacob than I like. Of the famous Old Testament twins I've always preferred Esau, with his impulsive appetites and his closeness to nature. Hunters, I always thought, are more glamorous than cultivators. Jacob was too calculating, too capitalist, too controlling, too patient in getting his own way. Yet even in Jacob there is a disarming vein of introspection and self-doubt. He wrestled with the Angel at Jabbok and was wounded, almost defeated by his own compulsions. But he never gave up on himself, was never entirely overwhelmed by his own desire to dominate. The Angel injured him in the thigh so that he limped, but he limped towards the sunrise.

[Originally published in *The Scotsman* on the 1st of January 1994.]

1   Bruce Chatwin: *What Am I Doing Here* (Picador, London).

Advent

ONE night before Christmas, when the house was quiet, I went into my study to prepare my sermon. On these occasions I normally sit in a large armchair for a preliminary think, moving to my desk only when I'm ready to put something down on paper. That's what I did. I settled into my large brown chair and started to think; and as I thought, I slept; and as I slept, I dreamt.

I saw my study with two men sitting in it. One was old and gentle, though at times he looked as commanding as an eagle. The other was much younger; he had a questioning, studious, rather restless face.

As I came in, the Elder was completing something he had just said to the young man. It was quite obvious to me that the studious young man was going to jump in immediately and say something. I thought I recognised familiar symptoms. He hadn't really been listening, or not wholeheartedly. Instead, he had been framing his reply, preparing his immediate rejoinder. I saw myself in that. Often, I don't really listen to people, I don't really let them disclose themselves because I'm so busy with my own responses to what they are saying. The young man was like that. He was already speaking.

'How can you, an educated man of the twentieth century, base your belief in what you call the divinity of Christ on a couple of first century legends, filled with angels who serenade shepherds abiding in the fields, mysterious strangers from the East who bring peculiar gifts to a babe lying in a manger, and messages from God that come in dreams?'

The old man replied: 'My dear, you are quite wrong if you think that the stories of the birth of Jesus are the basis on which we believe in him. How could they be? It is almost certain that the first generation of believers in Christ knew nothing at all about his birth. Paul, for instance, mentions the birth only once, and then with a complete absence of detail. There's no evidence that it was part of the early preaching of the Church at all. The trouble is that we have allowed the conventions of biography to influence our approach to these matters. We like things to start at the beginning and to come to an end. The frustrating thing about the early Christians is that they were not interested in playing that game at all! We don't find them talking about the unusual circumstances surrounding the birth of one who was now dead. They are just not interested in that.'

'Why not?' shot in the young man. 'The followers of a dead hero usually show an almost superstitious interest in the infancy details of their late leader.'

The old man smiled. 'When we first find the followers of *this* dead hero, they are busily proclaiming that he is not dead, that he is alive! That fact cancels out for them every other fact, including many that we'd love to know. They are just not interested in past biographical details because they are too busy proclaiming a present experience. This Jesus who was crucified, died and was buried, was not held by death. He rose again and lives still, so that men and women can know him now. You may not believe what they said, of course, but you must admit that if they believed it, it would make everything else, including details of Jesus' earthly life, seem insignificant.'

'I certainly can't believe that,' said the young man. 'I don't believe in miracles.'

'Ah,' said the old man, 'I thought that would be it.'

'Do you believe in miracles?' said the young man aggressively.

'No,' said the Elder, 'I don't believe in *miracles*. I believe in *God* and I have learnt after much pain and many false starts not to let my narrow idea of God limit God's freedom to act. Sometimes God acts in ways that shatter every human category and this places us in great danger. I've noticed, for instance, that when you're listening to me, you're not really paying complete attention. Oh, don't be embarrassed, it's a common human failing. Most of us do it. It's because we're only really convinced of our *own* existence, our own mental activity. Everything and everyone else is secondary, a walk-on part in the little soap opera of our life. That means they do not exist in freedom, they are there as cues or stimuli to our own little dramas. If we are not careful, we cease to pay attention to them, actually hear them, as they are in themselves, because we are locked into our own heads. We do this with God. Our idea of God, which is really a projection of our own mind, begins to take the place of the real God. Whenever God speaks or acts, what God says or does is monitored by this little-God-in-our-head, and if it does not conform to its preconceptions it is dismissed.'

The young man looked puzzled. 'What's the distinction between what you call our idea of God or the little-God-in-our-head, and what you call the real God? Is there any difference?'

'Oh, there's a great difference,' said the old man. 'It's the difference between your idea of a person before you've met, and the person as she really is.'

The young man still looked puzzled.

'Let me put it like this,' continued the Elder. 'Some sort of belief in God seems to be universal in time and place, with the possible exception of our own era. Philosophers have studied this mysterious fact. They ask: "How do you account for such an extraordinary idea and its extraordinary persistence?" Some have said that the only logical way to account for such a fact is by postulating a reality beyond us which presses its claim upon us. Some have investigated the mysteries of the human conscience, that strange conviction we have that good is to be preferred to evil; that peculiar outrage we feel at the triumph of wickedness; that sense we have that the saints of humanity are closer to the truth than the monsters of iniquity. How can you account for that mysterious sense of moral outrage if the universe is indifferent to value? Because, say the wise, there is a source of transcendent value beyond all of us which lays its claim upon each of us.

'But what are we left with? A hypothesis, a supposition, an idea!

11

Our mind has gone to work and it has produced a theory. If you stumble upon a carefully furnished cabin in a wood, you may logically conclude that someone lives there. But you do not know the owners just because you have inferred their existence. You have no relationship with them, unless they come to you, disclose themselves, come in the door and speak to you. Your mind has inferred the probability of their existence, but when they appear your preconceptions will be modified by reality, probably quite radically.'

'I can see that,' said the young man. 'I can see the difference between the idea of the owners and the owners themselves – but how can you apply that to God? Are you suggesting that God, like the cabin-owner, has appeared on the scene?'

'That's *just* what I'm suggesting,' replied the Elder. 'And why should this surprise you? You are letting your idea of God limit God's freedom if you deny the possibility of divine self-disclosure. If God there be, would it not be very strange if God did not seek us out? This process of divine self-disclosure is called by theologians "revelation", and it is the central category of all religion. The great prophets who have deepened our idea of God do not claim to have thought up something new: they claim to have heard a word of God.'

'I think I see what you're getting at,' responded the young man. 'These prophets who deepen our knowledge of God are a bit like musicians or artists of genius: something from outside, some extraordinary power or vision, seems to inspire them, to come through them. In a sense, then, God is working through them, putting a special pressure upon them, but it's still all at a first-remove. I'm prepared to concede that God can send messages, get through to mysteriously gifted people, but that's still a long way from saying God appeared or came in through the door of the cabin.'

'That's true,' said the Elder, 'but you've made an enormously significant leap. From a rather abstract idea of God, you have moved to the idea of a God who can act, who can press upon us. So imprisoned are we by the ideas of our mind that we often fail to hear other people. Just as tragically, we can fail to see and hear God. You know, that's what happened with Jesus. People just refused to hear him: "Is not this Joseph's son?" they said. "Someone we know" – thereby insulating themselves from the challenge he laid before them. That's what we do as well: keep him at a safe distance by coming up with alternative explanations.'

The young man broke in, 'How do *you* explain him? Are you saying that in Jesus, God, at last, came in the door? Are you saying that the God who spoke at various times and in various ways through the prophets from a distance, as it were, actually drew near, came close in Jesus? I'm afraid I find this both baffling and tantalising. Please try to explain. I mean, how could they have made this connection between Jesus and God?'

The old man replied: 'I know how difficult it is to grasp it, because the words we use have hardened into formula and abstraction, but it certainly was not like that for the first believers. The first followers of Jesus found that a gradual disclosure was being made to them. When they thought about it afterwards the only way they could find that at all fitted the experience was to say that they were having a close encounter with God in Jesus. It is very important to remember that the first disciples were Jews and, therefore, fanatically devout monotheists who had a horror of blasphemy and idolatry. They knew and obeyed the first commandment: "You shall have no other gods before me", yet they found themselves worshipping this man. Gradually, their ideas were all mixed up: God and this man became mysteriously equivalent. They started to feel an absolute loyalty to him. As philosophers might put it: he began to have for them the value of God. It was baffling. It called for a choice: either surrender to him or rejection of him. His first followers found themselves making the choice almost against their will. They were not imaginative men; not religious theorists given to sudden rushes of blood to the head. They were, in fact, slow of heart to believe. But the conviction forced itself upon them. They were progressively overwhelmed, not by a brilliant idea they had dreamed up, but by an overwhelming experience of God that came to them through this man. The gradual transvaluation was completed by the resurrection. The important and difficult thing to grasp is that the first Christians were not religious theorists who had dreamed up a new set of meta-physical ideas: they claimed only to be witnesses of the action of God. The long ages of silence were over. God who had in past ages spoken *through* the prophets had in these last days spoken *in* his Son, and that Son, now risen, was a living, energising presence who could be known by those who would open their hearts to receive him.

'That was the first message of the Church. You find it reflected in the New Testament letters, most of which were written long before the Gospels. Only later did they try to beat back upstream to the details of his birth, but the faith of the Church in Jesus is not founded upon them, though they are consistent with it. In these narratives you are given a picture of the coming of God to a darkened world that pays not the slightest attention. This is the theme of the great prologue to John's Gospel: the eternal coming of God to us, to God's own people, and their rejection of the divine stranger in their midst. One way or another that's what we still do. We're so pre-occupied, so self-obsessed, that we overlook the manifestation of God.'

The young man looked quieter but he was still very puzzled. 'How can I know all this is true? How can it be true for me?'

'You must believe before you can know,' replied the old man mysteriously. 'Oh, I'm not talking about a kind of mindless credulity. I'm talking about the most precious and difficult human action there is: the surrender and suspension of your own busy and self-important mental activity, the sheer noisiness of your mind, in order to let another be disclosed to you. I'm begging for a kind of inner silence so that another voice than your own might be heard, for it is only in silence that the gift is given.'

He sat back. 'I have failed, of course, to persuade you, but I never for a moment thought I might succeed. That was never my task anyway. I'm only here to ask for quiet, to hush you before the curtain is drawn back. God is his own witness and from all eternity he seeks you. God will not cease to seek an entrance to your life. You, too, feel the absolute nostalgia for God that is part of the human condition. It comes in those stabs of longing evoked by the sound of a treble voice in a dark church on a wild Christmas night. It comes

14

at all those brave and hopeless moments when we recognise the frailty and transience of what we have built our life upon. We're all homesick for God, yet too confused to recognise it. The message of this season is that God is coming after us. Jesus was called Emmanuel – God is with us – and God really does still come to those who will receive him. That's why we call our message good news.

'Leslie Weatherhead pointed out that good news is that which can be shouted across a street: "The war's over!" "The baby's born!" "Susan's out of danger!" "The strike's settled!" Well, here's my bit of good news for you: "God has come among you". All you have to do now is find the stable.'

*   *   *

And I woke with a start. 'All you have to do now is find the stable.'

Christmas Midnight

THERE was an optician's shop with a fancy window in our town. Behind the display area there was an arrangement of mirrors, so that if you passed the shop you saw yourself coming. The optician's was in Bank Street, next to the Strand Picture House, where I had spent many hours as a boy. Going to the pictures twice a week, as we did during the forties, was a great and pleasurable distraction. But we paid a price for it. The movies bred fantasy, unrealistic identification with the glamorous heroes of the silver screen. Gregory Peck was my undoing. A friend told my sister that she thought I looked like him, and in the screenplay that I was beginning to make of my life I became Gregory Peck in 'The Keys of the Kingdom', a film about missionary priests in China. This was the part I played until a March day in 1958 when I was walking down Bank Street. I had just returned from West Africa and fancied that the aura of missionary glamour still hung about me: a fading tan, a hint of resoluteness behind the ascetic features, and always, as far as women were concerned, a sense of seductive unapproachability. The illusion was shattered for ever outside the palace of fantasy that created it. I saw coming towards me a gangly, stick-like figure, with awkwardly receding hair, who gazed at me through national health specs fixed above a pointed, slightly skewed nose. 'Poor devil,' I thought, 'what a funny looking man.' A second later I realised that the optician's magic window was showing me myself as others saw me. Exit Mr Peck for ever.

If Hollywood was the main source of harmless fantasies, it was the Holy Catholic Church that instilled the dangerous illusions. As a boy at Kelham I was a compulsive consumer of lives of the saints, a literary genre that lacked psychological insight or any attempt to discover the humanity beneath the halo. One was never given any sense of struggle, nor any understanding of the intractable raw material from which the saint emerged. Instead, one was presented with a set of comic book virtues, remote from real human experience, with no redeeming shadow of vice. The temptation was to pick a role from Central Casting for Heaven and try it out, usually with no reference to one's own specific humanity.

The problem is that we spend much of our lives watching others and this leads to the theatricalisation of life, because watchers know they too are watched. And there are so many parts to play it takes time to discover who one is. I used to think this theatricalisation of life was a modern aberration, but I realise now it has always been a characteristic of human self-consciousness. Jesus told us two thousand years ago that there were certain religious types who did their acts of piety 'to be seen of men'. Even then life was cut into film clips and sound bites. Now, my fantasy of sanctity and sex appeal was manageable, not too tragic, and reality broke through without too much pain. Most of us fall into the amiable trap of imagining we possess the characteristics we admire in others and it's painful to own the truth about ourselves. It's altogether more difficult for those whose predicament is that they possess characteristics others abhor, a different thing entirely to the experience of *not* possessing characteristics people admire. These are the permanently despised minorities because, unlike most of us, they *are* different. Most people aren't handsome, after all, or holy, so they soon adjust to being neither. It's altogether different if you are a gay person in a society that will always be preponderantly straight, or a disfigured person in a society that worships beauty, or a depressive in a society that prizes optimism.

I realise now that in my life such people have ministered special grace to me, and the grace was not incidental to their condition but intrinsic to it. The confessors who have meant most to me have been gay priests with a profound sympathy for the waywardness and self-hatred of the human heart. Alcoholics have taught me most about personal honesty and reliance upon grace. Characteristic of all these people has been a refusal to collude with the conspiracy of success that characterises a moralistic church. They have rejected the bright and shining lie of human perfectibility and learned to live with only two certainties – their own frailty and the eternal forgiveness of Christ. Precariously, they live by grace and they minister it to others. By their wounds we are healed.

Increasingly, I understand the doctrine of the Incarnation in this way. The Word becomes flesh in all its uncertainty and awkwardness. Grace comes to us through weakness. The traditional account of the nativity, purged of its Christmas card glamour, captures the scandal of this paradox. There is the uncertainty that surrounds the conception. There is the confusion and incompetence that characterises the birth. Yet somewhere an angel sings, because God's grace has found another of the despised to dwell with. Grace uses every available weakness to pull down our might. It undermines the cruelty of our strength by throwing us on the mercy of our weakness. It is by our sin we are saved, because through it we reach for the grace that alone sustains us. This is why we should have a special regard for the despised, the little ones on the outside, the impure and the untogether. Not because they provide us with an opportunity for ministry, but because they afford us a means of grace. It is through them that God speaks to the Church. Through them the Church is evangelised.

I always enjoy Midnight Mass, because it is the one Church service the awkward squad turns out for with something like expectation. And I am always sad when I hear the preacher scold them for not coming since last year, not knowing the day of his visitation. Grace doesn't need protection, but it does require recognition. Titus reminds us every Christmas that 'the grace of God has dawned upon the world with healing for all'. Don't scold it when it comes. Let it bless you.

[Originally published in *Church Times*.]

18

Christmas Day

FROM time to time discoveries are made that greatly excite literary and artistic scholars. A hitherto unknown sonnet by Shakespeare is found or a youthful composition from the pen of Mozart is discovered and a scholarly debate ensues as to its authenticity. The same thing happens from time to time in the field of biblical studies. For instance, between 1947 and 1956 a collection of Hebrew and Aramaic documents was found in caves at Qumran, at the north western end of the Dead Sea. They provide first-hand evidence for Jewish life and thought at the time Jesus was born. Even more recently another discovery was made that has scholars in heated debate. It is an almost completely preserved manuscript that has been dated to about the year 70. Scholars disagree over its authenticity, but all agree that it is an interesting and remarkable document. It is a sort of autobiographical meditation written as an old man by Jonathan the son of Simon, inn keeper at Bethlehem at the beginning of the first century. An American Semitic scholar has made a modern paraphrase of the document and, instead of a sermon, I want to read what he has written, while cautioning you to remember that there are still many doubts about the authenticity of the document. Anyway, here's what Professor Capote has made of the manuscript.

*   *   *

'I, Jonathan son of Simon, of Bethlehem in Judaea, wish to set down my memory of events in my boyhood that are now being spoken of and written about, most recently in a strange text called "The Good

News", according to Luke, a physician, which has recently come to my attention. I am well beyond my allotted three score years and ten, but I can still remember the incident vividly. This is not due to any feat of memory; it is because the memory has never left me. I might almost say it has haunted me all my life.

'It is quite obvious to me that Luke does not intend to cast aspersions on my father in his account of the birth of Jesus of Nazareth, but I fear that his narrative has been interpreted in a way that places my father in a bad light, though he is not even mentioned in the text. In the first place, people ought to realise when they read the book of Luke that the so-called inn that Mary and Joseph came to was not the sort of place that modern readers imagine. It was a caravanserai, not a hotel, a square of covered stalls built round an open courtyard. Travellers who got there in time secured a place to camp under cover. They bedded the animals down in the centre of the courtyard. The innkeeper supplied a fire and feed for the beasts. Latecomers were never turned away – my father was a compassionate man – but if there was no room in the stalls they had to bed down in the open courtyard. That's what happened to Joseph and his wife. When they arrived the whole place was seething with people and animals and my poor father was harassed almost out of his mind. He was concerned for the young woman who stood silently by her husband. Neither of them complained, though Joseph did point out that his wife was having contractions. I was sent for clean straw and we made a space among the animals in which the young mother could lie down. I remember it because it was the first time I had been present at a birth. Mary wasn't that much older than me and I never forget a face.

'Her face I saw again many years later. My father was a shrewd businessman and we moved to Jerusalem where he secured the contract to provision the contingent of Roman soldiers permanently stationed in the city. When he died I took over and expanded the business. One Passover when Pontius Pilate was Governor of Judaea I had to supply an execution detail with wine. The Romans were pragmatic about such things. No soldier enjoyed the crucifixion detail and most of them only got through it if they were blind drunk. On the day in question my clerk had failed to supply sufficient wine and I myself had to bring another ten skins to Calvary at midday. There were three men hanging on crosses, the middle one strangely still in his agony. And that's when I saw her again. She was standing at the foot of the middle cross with a young man, both of them trying to hear what the man on the cross was saying. It was when they turned I remembered her from a lifetime away and I knew with absolute clarity that this blood-streaked figure was the baby who was laid in a feed box in the caravanserai at Bethlehem over thirty years before.

'Something went out of my life that day on Calvary. The woman was taken away by the young man before I could speak to her. What, anyway, would I have said? To be present at her son's birth and death and to know nothing else about him was disorientating, to put it mildly. It was only later I began to hear things about him and I still do not know what to make of them. There is a superstitious group of people abroad who claim that the birth and the death I witnessed were the work of God. The more fanciful among this group claim that this birth and death happened, in some sense, to God.

'It is a preposterous claim, of course, and I don't know why it troubles me, but trouble me it does. I have lost faith in religion but I am haunted by the possibility of God. Bethlehem and Calvary seem strangely characteristic of the God who haunts me. I want a proof, a powerful certainty; I want my mind to be overwhelmed by the obviousness of God. Instead, things turn up in my life, usually when I'm at my busiest, and they stand there on the edge of my consciousness, silent yet troubling. They have no power, these intimations, and they get there when the place is full up, every question answered, no room left for another possibility. What can this gentle disturbance be that goes on turning up on the edges of my life? Would God come like this, in weakness, making no attempt to capture my attention, so easily overlooked and

21

disproved, yet wounding me with longing that it might be so?

'I don't know how to answer these questions, but I know that each year about this time I go back to Bethlehem in my memory for a clue. Increasingly, Bethlehem and Calvary merge in my old man's memory and I know not whether it is birth or death I remember. I have noticed something else recently. If there is a God, and Bethlehem and Calvary are clues to that God's nature, then he won't overwhelm me; he is, in some sense, humble, ignorable almost by definition, subject to our arrogance and violence. To find such a God I, too, must stoop, climb down from all my pride and strength and go to him in weakness and trust. I have always been a proud man and find this kind of surrender difficult, so I remain for ever undecided, still the onlooker in the stable, the outsider on the hill. One day I pray that I may get closer to what I now think of as the pain of God. It is that time of year again. I remember my poor, too-busy father sending them into the courtyard and telling me to fetch some clean straw. Poor fools – they say it was the birth of God. I wonder – if I bent down and crept closer, as once I did as a boy, would God, at last, be born in me?'

[Originally used at St Mary's Cathedral, Edinburgh 1993. This sermon was published in *The Independent* in the week after Christmas 1993. One or two people wrote to me for details of the memoir mentioned in the sermon. I had to inform them that it was a preacher's invention.]

After Christmas

The shepherds said one to another, let us now go even unto Beth-
lehem and see this thing which has come to pass.   ~ Luke 2:15 ~

I'D like to know what happened to the shepherds after Christmas.
We can be fairly certain about what happened to the others. There
weren't many there, just enough to represent humanity; and we know
what happened to some of them. Mary and Joseph, for instance:
they were what we'd call naturally good, naturally religious people.
There are some in every generation: devout, unwavering in their
faith. We know what happened to Mary and Joseph after Christmas:
they stayed with Jesus, right up to the end. There are many who will
come to Bethlehem who won't go on to Calvary, but Mary did and we
can be certain that Joseph stayed beside her as long as he lived.
Mary ministered to Jesus at the joy of his nativity, and she was still
there, serving him at the sorrow of his crucifixion. So we know what
happened to Mary and Joseph. There are always some people whose
behaviour we can predict: their goodness is so fixed and settled, we
know how they'll react in a given situation. We can usually tell what
the truly devoted will do. Bethlehem and Calvary are all one to them.
Yes, we know what happened to Mary and Joseph after Christmas.

And we can be fairly certain about what happened to the three
wise men. The wise men were, like me, professional religious teachers.
There are always some in every generation: they are just naturally
interested in religious questions. Generally speaking, they are no
worse and no better than those who are not interested in religion.
They give their lives to the study of religion, fascinating as it is.

23

Sometimes they try to live it, but mainly they talk about it, make their living at it. It's their profession, after all. So we can be fairly certain about what happened to the wise men. They probably went back home and wrote up the experience and got it published. They'd lecture about it, give illustrated talks to the Women's Institute in Baghdad. They'd read papers about it all to the World Congress on Comparative Religion in Islamabad, and they'd be interviewed on Samarkand Television. After all, that's what professional wise men usually do. So we can be fairly certain about what happened to the wise men after Christmas.

But what happened to the shepherds? That's what I'd like to know. After all, they were the biggest group there, as they are the biggest group anywhere. They were the common people, neither particularly devout nor particularly interested in religion; working men, with little time to think about such things. Shepherds are usually very busy earning a living or enjoying what spare time they have. And we can be fairly certain how they behaved in Bethlehem. They'd stand around at the back, the way they do at weddings and baptisms, feeling slightly awkward and out of place, nipping out occasionally for a smoke. Perhaps they were impressed in spite of themselves, made uneasy by the sense that maybe there was something here they ought to be paying attention to, because it was mysteriously important. I like to think that at least one of the shepherds was permanently affected by that night and that he stood, strong and grieving, with the group at Calvary a lifetime later, and that he himself died on some alien hillside for the babe he saw born the night he watched in the fields above Bethlehem. I like to think that, and maybe it's true of one of them.

But I suspect it wasn't true for many of them. I think I know what happened to the shepherds after Christmas, because it happens year after year to most of us. After the temporary excitement and charm of it all we go back to our average ways. We remain unchanged. Bethlehem is nice once a year, but we are too booked up to go any further.

But why? Why is it so easy to remain unchanged, uninvolved? After all, we are not talking about some harmless and irrelevant

24

interest that has its strange enthusiasts. We are talking about the action and presence of Almighty God. We are talking about God whom one day, maybe one day soon, we shall confront with unavoidable finality. Of all things, then, why is it so easy to avoid him, to avoid the very reality that gives us the power of avoidance? Why is it so easy to be like the shepherds who went back to the price of wool and the cup final at Nazareth? Why is it so easy for us to live our lives as if the only thing that matters, because it holds all other matters in being, did not matter at all? The answer is simple. Is there, do you think, anything more helpless than a newborn baby? One thing, perhaps: a man nailed to a cross. Yet this is how God comes to us: in helplessness. He does not vanquish us with incontestable power; he presents himself in weakness and in silence. But why? Why does he make it so difficult: a baby in a manger, a man on a cross? Why like that? It's because he will not force us. He wants us to recognise him by our free choice; and because he is so quiet, it is easy to overlook him. Day after day he lays before us quiet and undemanding signs of his presence, wanting us to stay long enough to read them and recognise him and go to him at last. And most of the time we don't notice, we rush past.

Here tonight we're given another opportunity to meet him. Like the shepherds, maybe we've come for the excitement, the novelty. Perhaps some unbidden prompting has brought us, almost in spite of ourselves. Whatever the reason, here we are: in the dark and murmurous silence, caught for a moment slightly off guard.

I wonder what will happen to us after Christmas? Will tomorrow engulf us too soon and obliterate the memory of that unguarded moment just inside the shadow by the stable door? Or will tonight be our awakening, our moment of final recognition? Will we go with him beyond this night, or is this to be another of those one night stands that so characterise the lives of those who are too afraid or too confused to commit themselves? Time is getting on for all of us. I wonder what'll happen to us after Christmas?

[Originally used at St Salvador's, Edinburgh 1988.]

Epiphany

YOU will sometimes see this season described in prayer books as 'The Epiphany or Manifestation of Christ to the Gentiles'. As the title states, an epiphany is a manifestation, a revelation, disclosure, but there are different shades of meaning in the term. There is, for instance, something of the sense of a public exhibition or display, as in a show of presents before a wedding. Here you get a sense of untrammeled magnificence deigning to show itself to the public. In the epiphany of our Lord the uncreated glory of the everlasting God puts itself on display for our sake. But there is another, more insistent shade of meaning in this event. It suggests a secret power and glory which lies undetected and unregarded except to those with eyes to see. Many children's stories reflect an ancient fascination with power which is hidden and humbly disguised until some urgent event calls it forth. A slip of a girl is travelling alone in one of those old railway carriages that can only be entered when the train is stationary. Just as the train is pulling out, two large, evil-looking men enter the carriage and launch an attack upon the frail and defenceless girl. Of course, they don't know that she is the star pupil in the new martial arts programme at the local high school, and before they know what's happened to them they are begging for mercy as she unleashes her power, shows forth her prowess in the austere discipline of Kung Fu.

So then, in the epiphany of our Lord there is a disclosure, a revealing of something that lies hidden to the common gaze. We have to ask three questions, therefore:

- Where, and in what events, was the disclosure, the epiphany made?
- What, precisely, was revealed?
- What has it to do with me?

Before I offer an answer to those questions, let me remind you of a permanent element in Christian teaching. There is what we might call a sacramental dynamic at work in the Christian tradition. It shows itself, for instance, in the events of our Lord's life. These events have two layers of significance: there is the outward event and there is its inward meaning. We must not only ask, 'What happened?', but also 'What does it mean?' Again, these events are not to be taken as being purely historical, located only in the past. These are new kinds of events, which go on resonating in history; they are always contemporary for the believer, happening now. If that is not the experience of Christians, then it makes Christian doctrine arid; the doctrines are dead unless they live in us, in our experience. So, we'll look at the outward events, and we'll try to discover their inward meaning; and we'll seek to be faithful to the truths so revealed so that they can be made manifest in our own lives.

Let us, then, turn to the questions I asked. First of all, 'Where, and in what events, was the disclosure, the epiphany made?' Most people would immediately answer that by describing the coming of the wise men to Bethlehem to present gifts to the baby Jesus – gold and frankincense and myrrh. Well, that is probably the dominant element in the epiphany story, but there are two others – the baptism of our Lord by John, and our Lord's first miracle at Cana, where he changed water into wine and, as John describes it, 'manifested forth his glory'. Each of these events is seen as a disclosure, an epiphany, a showing-forth of something. The earliest office hymns for the Feast of the Epiphany tie all three together. Here are some verses from a fifth century hymn:

Lo, sages from the East are gone
To where the star hath newly shone:

Led on by light to light they press,
And by their gifts their God confess.

The Lamb of God is manifest
Again in Jordan's water blest,
And he who sin had never known
By washing hath our sins undone.

Yet he that ruleth everything
Can change the nature of the spring,
And gives at Cana this for sign –
The water reddens into wine.

If the revelatory events we are to contemplate on the Feast of the Epiphany are the coming of the magi, the baptism of our Lord in Jordan, and the first miracle that he wrought, at Cana in Galilee, we must ask next, 'What, precisely, was revealed?' The answer to that was well expressed in the fifth century hymn: 'Led on by Light to Light they press, and by their gifts their God confess.' It is divinity that is disclosed in these events, it is God who is manifested. This is the central claim of Christian Faith: in Jesus Christ God showed forth his glory, for our sake God conformed himself to our condition. Of course, no proof and little evidence can be presented to justify this claim. People come to a conviction about it not by argument but by inward assent. They come to it because something answers 'yes' from within. But there's always a mystery about it. The events that contain the epiphany can be looked upon with such a swift and careless gaze that they are never allowed to offer up their meaning. We become trapped by the narrowness of our seeing and the limits of our knowing. An Archbishop of Canterbury tells a story to illustrate this:

The story is told of one of my predecessors that he entered a railway carriage and took the last seat. In a few moments he realised that the other passengers in the carriage were from the local mental

hospital. He buried himself in his papers, but suddenly the carriage
door was thrust open and an official began counting, 'One, two,
three, four .... Who are you?' 'I am the Archbishop of Canter-
bury.' 'Five, six, seven, eight ....' [1]

The divine nature of Jesus Christ, the doctrine of the Incarnation,
that God became flesh in a Jew from Nazareth, raises acutely the
most offensive element in Christianity, what C H Dodd called 'the
scandal of particularity'. Most people can accept some generalised
form of Theism. As they say, 'they believe God exists'. What offends
them about Christianity is its assertion that this remote and generalised concept of distant divinity actually invested itself in a particular life at a particular place in a unique and particular way. Again,
there is little point in arguing about it. What court on earth could
possibly judge a claim like that? No, people are not argued into
faith in Christ. When faith comes it is the response to an epiphany,
a disclosure, and it is difficult to describe it in prose. Music and
poetry capture it best. Here is a bit of a poem that seems to me to
capture something of the process of recognition that goes on, as
well as providing an insight into the scandal of particularity. It comes
from a poem called 'The Return of Arthur' by Martyn Skinner.[2] An
unbeliever finds himself entranced in a church, gazing at a wooden
plaque of the Nativity.

So Leo gazed, absorbed, a timeless glance;
And thought of all the trees that nature held
(Strange instance of a trance within a trance);
Cedars of Lebanon, green beechwoods delled
With sapphire; sombre newsprint forests felled
    At such a rate, each Sunday men were able
    To read ten acres at the breakfast table;

Dwarf fairy oaks at Lichen, harled with moss;
Trunks wide as roads, through which a cart could go;
A jungle mat a continent across

Which, piled as logs, would make the Alps look low –
And yet of all that ever grew, or grow
    (So ran his thoughts) this carving had been done
    Uniquely from a random plank of one.

Was not the contrast much the same in space,
Whose glittering forests were the galaxies?
For if the carver made a special case,
Selecting from innumerable trees
One segment, so from the vast host of these
    Could not the prime Creator, mightier far,
    Have carved his story on a single star?

And if he had, Ah, if indeed he had,
And come himself to earth, a newborn cry,
Would not the story have been just like that;
And signs accompanied, in earth and sky,
That holy abdication from on high;
    And radiant beings from about the throne
    Of light, have made the lamplit stable known?

Well, if these events in the life of Jesus disclose something of the meaning of 'that holy abdication from on high', what do they mean for me? How are they to be made manifest in my life? That is a question each of us must ask, and each must answer. Speaking personally, these modes of epiphany, of divine disclosure, suggest three related things to me.

The adoration of the magi speaks of self-surrender. I must seek to present myself, my soul, my body to Christ.

But I don't find this easy, so the baptism of our Lord suggests another element. The shadow of the cross lies over that baptism. Our Lord was commissioned to a ministry that led to death. My discipleship means not only generalised self-surrender, it must also mean quite particular self-denial. There is that in me which must be denied, suppressed. But that is not the final note.

The wedding at Cana suggests that Christ wishes to increase my joy, so I find in him self-fulfilment as well as self-denial.

As I contemplate the Epiphany and its meaning, therefore, it speaks to me of self-surrender, self-denial and self-fulfilment. My journey into the meaning of Christ brings joy *and* discipline, and I dare not have one without the other. The Epiphany of our Lord Jesus Christ is both gift and demand. The glory of the love that is revealed wakes in me a longing to give back love for love. It is difficult, I know, but 'Love so amazing, so divine, demands my life, my love, my all'.

[Originally used at St Mungo's, West Linton 1988.]

1   Told by Archbishop Robert Runcie.
2   Martyn Skinner: 'The Return of Arthur', from Austin Farrer: *A Celebration of Faith* (Sermons).

Windows on the Passion

(i) JOHN 13:21-30

EACH Holy Week I wait with a sort of premonitory shiver for three little words from John's Gospel chapter 13, the story we have just listened to. It tells of that strange, cryptic dialogue between Jesus and Judas. Jesus knows what Judas is about to do and Judas knows that Jesus knows, but the other apostles gathered there remain blissfully unaware of the impending tragedy. Maybe Jesus was making a last minute appeal to Judas to change his mind, or maybe he had recognised that the die was cast, the engine of betrayal was running. However we explain it, the motives of Judas will always be a mystery. He leaves the upper room, leaves Jesus and his companions, the friends he worked and shared with, and goes towards his tragic destiny. John tells us that he went out and 'it was night'. These are the words that always send a little shiver up my spine. It was night. They are not accidental words thrown in as a sort of time check. John is a writer who piles layers of meaning into the simplest words, and this is the case here.

Some years ago a remarkable book was written by a theologian called Bill Vanstone, with a strange and arresting title, *The Stature of Waiting*.[1] And these little words were important to the theme he addressed in that book. He reminded us that Jesus had said during the time of his active ministry that he worked like his heavenly father, and he went on to say 'work while it is day for the night comes when no one can work'. In other words, there was an intensely active phase in Jesus' life and ministry, but there came a point when activity ceased and he began to be acted upon. He worked while it was the day time of his ministry, but the night came when he had to give up his work and be acted upon. 'Judas went out and it was night.' Jesus now reached the moment of surrender, the moment when there would be nothing he could do, no active steps he could take. Instead he would become a patient, someone who is acted upon, someone who waits for others to decide what is to happen. If you've been in hospital you'll know exactly how this feels. We call people who are treated in hospital 'patients', and the word is highly appropriate. It requires immense patience to be in hospital, to wait upon the decisions of doctors, of surgeons, to wait for the result of tests, to wait for that word from the consultant who stands at the foot of your bed. There is not much you can do except trust in their skill and compassion and surrender yourself to their healing care. Bill Vanstone called his book *The Stature of Waiting* because he believed that we, in our over-activity, did not pay sufficient regard to the importance of waiting in our lives; the power it has, the opportunity it provides; these times of waiting, these times when we are patients. The times when events have been taken out of our control can be deeply enriching as we surrender ourselves, say Yes to what is happening and allow God to carry us through them.

That is certainly what John is suggesting Jesus did. The day had passed. The day in which he had taught and healed and worked wonders and strode about Judea surrounded by needy people: that day was now over. He would now do his mightiest work by a kind of dynamic inactivity, a passionate waiting, a final surrender to God.

It's a theme that seems to preoccupy John, because he returns to it at the end of his Gospel, this time when Jesus is speaking to Peter: 'Truly, truly, I say to you when you were young you girded yourself and walked where you would. But when you are old you will stretch out your hands and another will gird you and carry you where you do not wish to go.' It is the same theme. The day is over. The night of waiting has come. But the point to recognise is that it is precisely at this moment that God can come close to us and carry us because we are no longer able to walk by ourselves.

After receiving the morsel
Judas immediately went out;
and it was night.

* * *

(ii) MARK 14:32-42

I'VE already pointed out that I'm deeply moved every Holy Week by the little words 'and it was night', but I'm equally moved by the story of our Lord's watching in the Garden of Gethsemane. The Gethsemane story is about the brave acceptance of reality and for me, again, the most potent phrase is very simple. Jesus goes to the disciples and addresses them: 'Are you still sleeping and taking your rest? It is enough. The hour has come.'

The hour has come. Jesus recognises irresistible necessity, the thing that could not be altered. There are times in our lives when we have to admit to a cruel, sometimes terrifying certainty that we cannot escape from. These are the hours when darkness reigns and absolute honesty and courage are required of us. We have to know what's on the X-ray the doctor is bringing into the consulting room, because we have to deal with reality and not fantasy. We need to know the truth about ourselves, however unpalatable it is, when we are told it in love by our partners or friends. Many of us spend our lives denying the truth about ourselves, running from reality, from the way we really are. We prefer consoling fantasies to reality. But this means that we never truly live, because we are always in flight from reality. Facing the truth, though painful, is the first step to dealing with reality. Sometimes we have to say the words to ourselves: I am dying of cancer; my marriage is in trouble; I am an alcoholic; I am gay. Whatever reality we have been in flight from we have to face, as Jesus faced his betrayers in the Garden of Gethsemane. Life brings these betrayals: lovers turn from us, society discards us, our own

34

bodies betray us and there is no escape. There is no secret passage-way out of the Garden of Gethsemane. There is no regiment of angels that will suddenly blast its way into our midst and rescue us. There is only the raw fact that our betrayer is at hand and since there is no escape from the event, meaning has to be found within the event. Since the betrayal cannot be undone, we have to allow our human-ity to transcend it, even as the betrayer kisses us. This is easy to say, difficult to do. We do not want this reality that confronts us, this death, this loss, this ending of our working life. These things *are* betrayals and they should not happen. God should do something about them. This is what we feel as anger and panic rise in our throat. But the fact remains that these things do happen. Judas is constantly bringing the police into our garden of contentment to drag us away and we must deal with the situation that faces us, not waste energy wishing it away. The peace that lies on the other side of the horror can only be reached by going through the experience to the other side. Somehow we have to say Yes to it, look it in the eye and acknowledge it. When they came for Jesus he began his triumph over the betrayal by standing erect and going with his captors in proud submission to whatever awaited him.

It is enough. The hour has come.

* * *

(iii) LUKE 22:54-62

IT'S the simple words in the Passion narratives that get to me. 'It was night.' 'The hour has come.' And in this tragic passage from Luke come some of the most poignant words in the New Testament. They tell the story of Peter's betrayal of Jesus. It's important to under-stand what this betrayal is about. Peter wasn't a cynical double-agent planted among the followers of Jesus in order to deliver him into his enemies hands. He loved Jesus. He meant it when he said he would follow him to death. He was not lacking in impulsive courage, but in many ways he was a weak man. That's why I identify with him, because I, too, have ideals that I've failed, promises that I've broken; so I can understand how Peter felt in that terrible moment in the courtyard as he was challenged by the servants of the High Priest. Even as he denied Jesus he was loving him, and filling himself with shame and self-loathing. When we are most unsure of ourselves we become most vehement and passionate, as did Peter here. 'I know not the man.' And immediately the cock crows, and then the terrible, wrenching words: 'And the Lord turned and looked at Peter. And Peter remembered the word of the Lord, how he had said to him, "Before the cock crows today you will deny me three times". And he went out and wept bitterly.'

Why did he weep? Most certainly out of shame, remorse, repentance and self-loathing; but I think it was Jesus' look that really made him weep, because it wasn't a look of hatred or contempt or disgust; it was an unbearable look of love. Even as Peter denied him, Jesus was forgiving him. Forgiveness like that is almost unbearable for us. Most of us know deep inside ourselves what we are like. We don't feel terrific about ourselves, wish we were stronger. But we are insecure, full of self-doubt, so we react to criticism, attack an accusation defensively – we bluster, deny reality, resist the criticism. I certainly do. I hate criticism. Something in me always jumps to my own defence – it's so instinctive I can hardly help it. Peter was like that, too; he was a bit of a blusterer who reacted badly to criticism. But he doesn't bluster here, he weeps; he doesn't defend himself, he breaks down in sorrow and repentance; and not because Jesus challenges him, 'I told you so, I knew you'd let me down'. No, what broke Peter down was that look of love. What he couldn't bear was the pity, the compassion in the eyes of Jesus, who knew and loved Peter and felt the pain, the shame, the self-loathing his old friend was going through. It's love, forgiving love, that breaks us down and changes us. That's what Peter saw in the look of Jesus.

And this is what the Cross means. Nothing can separate us from the divine love, even our own squalid little betrayals, our own denials. No one has put it better than Austin Farrer:

> *God forgives me with the compassion of his eyes, but my back is turned to him. I have been told that he forgives me, but I will not turn and have the forgiveness, not though I feel the eyes on my back. God forgives me, for he takes my head between his hands and turns my face to his to make me smile at him. And though I struggle and hurt those hands – for they are human, though divine, human and scarred with nails – though I hurt them, they do not let go until he has smiled me into smiling; and that is the forgiveness of God.*[2]

And the Lord turned and looked at Peter.

* * *

(iv) MATTHEW 27:31*b*-50

IN that marvellous quotation above from Austin Farrer we are told that as we struggle we hurt the wounded hands of God. He told us they are 'human, though divine, human and scarred with nails'. The Christian Gospel is about forgiveness, but it is not about cheap forgiveness. It costs God dear. It scars his hands with nail wounds. God's love for us and forgiveness of us are not evidence of an easy-going indifference to our betrayals. He doesn't offer us cheap grace. In my life as a preacher I have often preached forgiveness as though it were an easy matter. It's not. God is not indifferent to our follies. He's not a lazy or indulgent parent who spoils his children because he cannot stir himself out of his own preoccupations and wants to buy peace for himself. God's forgiveness comes from his passionate love and it is that same love that is the source of his pain. I'm very fond of another quote, this time from a Frenchman called Charles Peguy. He said, quite rightly, 'The sinner is at the heart of

Christianity. No one understands Christianity better than the sinner'.[3]

If you identify with Peter, as I do, you will understand these words. We are not necessarily bad people, but we are often weak people who fail our own ideals and what breaks our heart is not the condemnation of God, but God's great love shown in the Cross. It is very hard for theologians to say exactly how we are saved by the Cross of Christ, but one of the theories that has always attracted me is called the Exemplarist theory, and I apologise for the technical term. It simply means that the death of Jesus sets before us an example of the divine love and moves our imagination and will to repentance and holiness. As we gaze upon the crucified, as we survey the wondrous Cross, our hearts are touched by God's pain, God's pity, God's suffering love, and we are changed by it. Loved like that, how can we bear not to love in return; forgiven like that, how can we refuse to forgive others. So the example of the love of God and the patience and suffering of Christ draw us to the life of holiness, the life of surrender. I've already quoted Peguy as saying that the sinner is at the heart of Christianity, but he goes on to say, 'No one understands Christianity better than the sinner. No one, unless it be the saint'.

That captures the whole meaning of the Passion of our Lord. He died for sinners like you and me, but he longs to make us into saints.

[Originally used on BBC Scotland, Palm Sunday 1994.]

1   Bill Vanstone: *The Stature of Waiting* (Darton, Longman and Todd: London).
2   Austin Farrer: *Said or Sung* (Faith Press, 1960).
3   Quoted as the epigraph on Graham Greene's novel, *The Heart of the Matter*.

Maundy Thursday: Liturgy of the Chrism

Am I now seeking the favour of men or of God? Or am I trying to please men? If I were still pleasing men I should not be a servant of Christ.   ~ Galatians 1:10 ~

PAUL has put his finger here on the most frustrating and irritating aspect of the life of the ordained minister. Most other jobs have an objectivity about them which enables us to separate the people from the work they do: lawyers, plumbers and gas persons can all be splendid practitioners of their various crafts; they can be good at their jobs, while leading selfish and disordered lives. Indeed Bishop Hensley Henson once said that he'd rather employ an efficient plumber who was a rogue than a saintly incompetent. But it is not so with ordained ministers. There is, of course, a proper professionalism about which we are all beginning to learn, a proper competence, a proper regard for the right use of our time and carefulness in the objective administrative tasks that fall to us, as well as a proper professionalism in our leading of worship. Nevertheless, the nature of the ministry is never fully expressed by competence or professionalism and this is because the instinct of ordinary people is to judge us less by what we say or do, or by the way we perform, than by what we are in ourselves. There is no private zone, no area that is not in some sense part of the manner of our ministry. We are not professionals who can keep our lives in two compartments; we are, in Paul's words, 'servants or slaves of Christ', and slaves had no private identity apart from what they did. They didn't work at slavery from nine to five – they *were* slaves. Slavery, like marriage, is what the Prayer Book calls an estate, a state of being. We don't have to accept a High Church theology of ministerial succession to understand this. Even if we have a mainly functional understanding of ministry, most of us recognise that there is a strongly representative aspect to our role, which is one reason why clergy who get into trouble are of great interest to newspaper editors. And it is this which imposes the greatest anxiety upon us because, in the eyes of the world, we are given over totally to the service of Christ. In all sorts of ways and in all sorts of places the Church, indeed Christ himself, will be judged by what we are. Our dilemma is that, knowing this, we also know how weak and selfish we are; how feeble our spiritual life is. We know the gap between the public expectation and the private reality; the gap between the knowledge of what we long to be and what we actually are. We often feel in our hearts that we are figures of contradiction, tragic clowns, like the ones in Kierkegaard's parable, who ran through the town telling people that the circus tent was on fire, but everyone just roared with laughter at what they thought was brilliant clowning – and the circus was destroyed. We are seriously intent on proclaiming a message which is often obscured by our own nature and its limitations. We are clowns, suddenly made the guardian and proclaimer of momentous tidings, and people cannot hear what we say because they think they know what we are.

This is why ministers of the Gospel, like all the best clowns, usually have their hearts broken by the very nature of what they are called to do. Michael Ramsey used to point out in his ordination charges that priests were no good until their hearts had been broken. Only when they have grieved over the impossible predicament that they are in and tasted the bitterness and scandal of the fact that they, as they know themselves truly to be, are nevertheless stewards of the mystery of Christ; only then will the contradiction, the split in their own lives become fruitful for good, as they implore God to fill their unrighteousness with Christ's goodness, their impurity with Christ's love, their selfishness with Christ's spirit of self-offering. 'A broken and a contrite heart, O Lord, thou wilt not despise.'

So, first and foremost, ministers of the Gospel must be penitents. Any minister who is not a penitent is failing to discover the heart of ministry. There are various ways of expressing the penitential life, but all of them are based upon the need to grow in self-understanding, self-knowledge; the need to live what Plato called 'the examined life'. This can be done very privately, or can be done – perhaps *ought* to be done, at least on occasions – with the help of a friend in the Lord, who will rescue us from unnecessary self-abasement or unnecessary self-delusion. What seems to me to be inescapable is the need to grow in true knowledge of the self, and this is not simply a matter of going through a checklist from time to time of the things we have done that we ought not to have done, or things we have left undone. That is usually the *easiest* part of self-knowledge. More difficult is understanding the kind of people we are. Here we can easily flee from true knowledge of ourselves; we can dismiss it as psycho-babble or navel-gazing, and take refuge in things that genuinely need to be done. But how can we genuinely minister to people if we are not, at least to some extent, aware of the inner dynamics of our own nature, the effect we have on other people, our own inner fears, needs, insecurities, longings – especially the unadmitted or unacknowledged ones.

This truth in the inward parts is a very important element in spiritual leadership. If I do not understand or admit the truth about myself, how can I help to lead others to the knowledge of the truth about themselves, or, more profoundly, the truth of the mystery of the invisible God? The nature of ministry is *incarnational.* God uses the givenness of our human reality to reveal himself, express himself to the world. But our given nature modifies and distorts that revelation, and part of our vocation is to submit to a process of purification that allows God to increase and our interruptions of his revelation to decrease. The paradox is, of course, that the more we dispose ourselves to the divine use in this way, the more like our real selves we become. There are many human models of the ministry. Indeed, they are probably as numerous as personality types. I would like to look at three fairly common clergy models and ask a few questions about how each type might grow in self-knowledge and might dispose itself more perfectly to the will of God.

One of the most basic or classic models of ministry is that of the rebel or non-conformist. There is always, of course, much that is corrupting and oppressive in the life of the Church in the world, and therefore much to be rebelled against; so we need our rebels. However, the rebels need to know themselves, unless they are simply to use the ministry as a way of indulging or expressing unresolved tensions in their own inner nature. Rebels need to distinguish between a desire to shock and offend for its own sake, and the duty to challenge the complacency and thoughtlessness of others. How much of my rebelliousness comes from God and his controversy with the world, and how much comes from my own immaturity?

If the rebel is a common clerical type, the scold is even more common. Clerical scolds, like sheepdogs, are constantly snapping at the heels of their parishioners, trying to drive them this way or that, rarely letting them be, unable to let them graze in peace or wander at will. Scolds are usually driven by an inordinate sense of responsibility that makes them tense and sometimes unapproachable. Their conscientiousness and seriousness, which are their greatest virtue, are also the source of their greatest weakness. Ministers are called on occasion to admonish and exhort, to be challenging and prophetic, but it is also possible that they are doing these right things for the wrong reason; so scolding clerics need to ask themselves why they don't trust their congregations, why they are constantly getting at them, and what kind of God it is who drives them. If rebels often need to grow up, scolds need to learn how to relax – unlike the third type, who is probably too relaxed.

This is what we might call the lay model of the ministry: the minister who is one of the boys, or one of the girls, uneasy with the clerical state, anxious not to be too identified with it, and very keen to demonstrate his or her humanity. Well, clergy like that are frequently very attractive, especially to the worldly, and they witness against the evil of the ministry forming itself into some kind of Brahmin cast. Nevertheless, ministers who take this line have to ask themselves if they are not perhaps afraid of some of the responsibilities ordination has imposed upon them; are they not trying to have their cake and eat it; and they have to ask whether their ministry lacks edge and commitment.

The point I'm trying to make in all this is that we need our rebels, our scolds and those who are so laid back they are almost horizontal, and God uses them *all*. But if it is God we are serving and not ourselves, if we are not simply using the ministry as a way of expressing our own personality, then we have to ask ourselves profound and probing questions about the way in which we minister. And this need not be a heavy or guilt-ridden process. Self-discovery can be as exciting as any other kind of discovery. As we renew our ordination vows today, let us recommit ourselves to the examined life, the penitent life, and ask God, not only that we may increase in knowledge of him, but that we may increase in knowledge of ourselves.

[Originally used at St Mary's Cathedral, Edinburgh 1989.]

Trying the Resurrection:
A Courtroom Drama

... but in your hearts sanctify Christ as Lord. Always be ready to make your defence to anyone who demands from you an accounting for the hope that is in you.

~ I Peter 3:15, *New Revised Standard Version* ~

SPEECH FOR THE PROSECUTION

Ladies and Gentlemen:

THE Resurrection of Jesus Christ is the cornerstone on which the whole of Christianity is built. If it is false, the entire edifice collapses. The Resurrection is what Christians call a miracle. What is a miracle? A miracle is an event for which, it is claimed, there is no natural explanation and which is, therefore, held to have been performed by God. Now, belief in miracles was understandable in an age that knew nothing of science and little of the workings of nature. The miraculous was used to fill up gaps in human knowledge in the pre-scientific era. We no longer need this supernatural explanation. We now understand the way nature works. The gaps in our knowledge have been filled. We now know that everything that happens has a natural cause. What was a miracle to our forebears is now seen by us to be the working of the laws of nature. If we examine the alleged evidence for the Resurrection of Jesus from the dead, we shall see that it can be explained perfectly well without resorting to a miraculous act of God.

44

The Christians make two claims. First, the tomb of Jesus was found to be empty. Second, Jesus himself appeared to his disciples three days after his execution.

The empty tomb need not delay us long. The mere absence of a corpse proves nothing. The dead man's followers could easily have removed it and conveniently disposed of it.

And the evidence of the appearances is equally dismissible. These can be explained on a simple, psychological basis. The disciples were probably quite sincere victims of hallucination. Being unequipped with our knowledge of the workings of the human mind and its ability to project mental expectations in what appears to be an objective form, they would naturally interpret these hallucinations as the actual bodily appearances of their dead leader.

Finally, it is worth pointing out that the Christian records of this supposed event are inconsistent and contradictory. In Matthew, a single angel rolls back the stone and greets the ladies at dawn. In Mark, 'a man' dressed in a white robe informs them that Jesus is risen. In Luke and John, however, it takes two heavenly messengers to make the announcement. Moreover, in Matthew and Mark the women who first discover this Resurrection are bidden by the risen Jesus to tell the disciples to go into Galilee where he will meet them. Luke and John know nothing of this excursion. In their accounts Jesus meets his disciples in and around Jerusalem.

I call upon you, therefore, to dismiss the Resurrection as a pious fable, which its most committed and articulate protagonists could not even clothe with consistency. Jesus Christ did not rise from the dead. Rational minds can reach no other verdict.

SPEECH FOR THE DEFENCE

THE case against the Resurrection is based not on argument or explanation, but on a large and untested assumption. Let me give you an illustration. In the middle ages most people believed that the earth was flat. When scientists offered evidence to prove that it was in fact round, their evidence was rejected, not because it was proved to be false, but because people had already made up their minds on the subject. It is the same with the miraculous. If you have made up your mind that miracles can't happen, then no amount of evidence will persuade you otherwise. But that doesn't mean you're right. It merely proves that you are in the grip of a very powerful prejudice, or *pre*-supposition. You pre-judge the evidence; you *pre*-suppose the conclusion. Suppose a momentous miracle had occurred, how could you know about it if you dismiss the very possibility as absurd?

I want to offer you another definition of a miracle. A miracle is the interruption of a law of nature by a higher law, which we may not yet understand. Every time an aeroplane flies through the air without falling to the earth, it is a kind of miracle. There is a law of nature called the Law of Gravity and by that law the plane ought to fall. But it doesn't, because a higher law has supervened and altered the course of nature. That higher law is the human mind, which, in turn, has discovered the laws of aerodynamics. Every day we hear of new miracles of science – new ways in which humanity defies and alters the course of nature. If the laws of nature can be interfered with by the human mind, why can't they be interrupted by a higher power than human reason, a higher purpose – the mind and purpose of God himself? Why is it judged incredible with you that the God who created life should also be able to raise the dead?

Now let us look at the evidence. The empty tomb. The idea that our Lord's disciples stole the body is unbelievable. The very existence of this same theory in Jerusalem at the time is itself an interesting piece of evidence in support of the empty tomb, but it is psychologically absurd to think the disciples could have stolen the body. Their whole conduct forbids us to regard them as imposters. Why should they persist in a deception that brought them nothing but danger and death? Would St Peter have gone to a martyr's death in Rome for the sake of a deception which he himself had perpetrated? A plot like this is always betrayed in the long run and wilful fraud is utterly inconsistent with the lives of the disciples.

More plausible is the suggestion that the disciples were sincere, but were the victims of hallucination. But this won't stand either. Such hallucinations obey certain general laws. For instance, they all imply expectation. People see what they want to see. But all the evidence shows that our Lord's friends, so far from expecting a resurrection, were actually preparing to embalm a corpse. The appearances of our Lord were totally unexpected and were, at first, received with disbelief by the disciples. Such lack of faith is hardly likely to be an invention. It cannot be said that modern psychology lends any support to this view, when the facts are tested.

Both of these interpretations of the evidence must be ruled out of court. But the main piece of evidence has not so far been hinted at. This is the evidence of the existence of the Church, in spite of the catastrophe of Good Friday. You must ask yourselves: what happened to change the male disciples from crushed and broken men, men who forsook their Lord at the time of danger; what happened to change them into men who suddenly started preaching him whom they had only just denied? What happened to change them into men who could face death and imprisonment with untroubled courage? What happened to enable them to turn the biggest tragedy of their lives into a gospel that turned the world upside down and is still being preached today? We cannot avoid those questions. We cannot avoid the existence of the Christian Church. Only a momentous and shattering event could have turned that band of dispirited Galilean peasants into a generation of heroes who changed history. If Christ be not risen, the Christian Church is based on a colossal lie and her preaching is false.

Yet it was this lie, apparently, which turned the world upside down. This lie changed the face of history. For the sake of this lie Stephen was stoned to death in Jerusalem and Peter and Paul were crucified in Rome. And since that time, this, the greatest lie in history, has sent countless Christian martyrs to death, calling on the name of the Risen Lord. This lie has sent out numberless heroes into the world to spend themselves in love and service to others. This lie has inspired some of humanity's greatest art. This lie has quieted the hearts of countless people in the face of the terrors of death, because they knew their Lord had gentled death and made it the gate to life eternal.

Can you possibly believe that a deception perpetrated in an obscure Roman outpost two thousand years ago could have worked all this? And what incompetent deceivers they were! My learned friend has already pointed out to you the inconsistencies and contradictions in their own written evidence. Is that kind of thing the mark of clever deceivers? Would not real deceivers have smoothed the inconsistencies out, put together a single version of events, instead of delivering their candid but confused memories of the event to a scoffing world? It is this very naivete which is their strongest claim upon our trust, because deceivers do not thus act, but the honest do. Ask any ten honest people to describe an event they all witnessed, and you'll get ten different versions. Ask ten criminals for their account of a crime they were all implicated in, and you'll get a single, neat explanation. The truth is always untidy, while lies come neatly wrapped. No, my friends, the Resurrection is one of the most thoroughly and dramatically attested facts in history. Christ is indeed risen from the dead. Indeed, he is present with us today. We will perceive him in our midst if only we will open ourselves to his presence.

Today in this Church there are many people. Some have recently lost husband or wife, father or friend, in death. Some are troubled by a particular problem, a personal weakness, a decision that has to be taken. Some are infrequent Church-goers, not sure whether they believe, yet not entirely satisfied with a life that is spiritually empty. All sorts and conditions of men and women. And this, the Queen and First and Best of days, is their day. Whatever the need, on this day it can be met. Heartbreak can be healed by this day. On this day weakness can find strength. And on this day all searching ends. For this is the day which the Lord has made. This is the day of Resurrection. For Christ our Lord is risen. Let us rejoice and be glad.

[Originally used at Church of the Advent, Boston, Easter 1983.]

Pentecost

THIS is a day that has two names. The older name is Pentecost, a Greek word that means 'the fiftieth day'. Pentecost was the festival in the Old Testament when the first fruits of the corn harvest were presented and it fell fifty days after the Passover. The Christian Church has always tried to stress the continuity between itself and other religious traditions it has built upon. So, rather than abandoning Jewish feasts, it has adapted them to its own purposes and uses, and has done the same thing with many of the old pagan festivals and pagan sites of worship. Our Pentecost comes fifty days after our Passover, and there's an old hymn that captures it exactly: *'For since the Resurrection Day, a week of weeks had passed away.'* The other name for this feast is Whit Sunday, derived from the days when those who had been baptised into the Christian Church at Easter wore their white baptismal robes to church on the Feast of Pentecost or White or Whit Sunday.

So much then for the name and how we got it. What about the extraordinary events recorded in the Acts of the Apostles where we read that 'the Church was gathered together on the Feast of Pentecost and the Holy Spirit fell upon the assembled company, who broke into tongues'. And we are told foreign visitors to Jerusalem for the Feast heard uneducated Galileans speaking under the influence of the Spirit in their own language. Some interpreters of this event are profoundly embarrassed by it and they try to turn it into an allegory. They say that Luke, the author of the Acts of the Apostles, intends us to interpret his description as a piece of code. One of the favourite methods of interpreting Luke's story is to see it as an echo of the

49

story of the building of the tower of Babel in the Old Testament. God gets angered and frightened by the arrogance of humanity trying to build a tower to heaven, so he divides them into different language groups so that they can no longer co-operate with one another. The diversity of languages becomes a symbol of human arrogance and disunity. But here on the Feast of Pentecost that division is reversed into the spiritual unity of the universal Church, one gospel for one world.

Well, that is a fruitful method of meditation but there is no need to be embarrassed by the supernatural events that Luke described because they are still experienced today. Under the influence of what is called the charismatic or neo-pentecostal movement, the experiences described in the second chapter of the Acts of the Apostles are familiar to many people today, though there is no agreement on explaining the phenomenon, or even evaluating its significance. There are many modern examples of people praying in tongues under the influence of intense religious fervour. We have to make a distinction within that phrase – praying in tongues – because it covers two separate experiences called *Zenolalia* and *Glossolalia.* Zenolalia, speaking coherently in a foreign language one does not know, is what is described in the Acts of the Apostles, where the first Christians speak in the language of the Parthians, the Elamites and dwellers in Cappadocia, and so on. Accounts are given by modern pentecostalists of this very experience. I have read stories of well-known Christians who have found themselves praying in a language they themselves did not understand, being approached afterwards by foreigners who told them that they had just recited the Lord's Prayer in Mandarin Chinese, or a little known African dialect. Zenolalia is rare. Glossolalia is much more common. It is really just an ecstatic noise that can sometimes be very beautiful and sometimes rather comical. I had personal experience of it. I found myself praying in tongues 20 years ago and found great spiritual refreshment from the experience. I still occasionally use this way of praying, especially if I am giving the laying-on of hands for healing and don't know exactly what to say.

A friend of mine described this type of praying as silent prayer that makes a noise, partly because it probably has no meaning except the desire to praise God or express love or longing. It is a kind of verbal music.

You can accept these phenomena without rating them particularly highly. Paul certainly knew they happened and he had to tell enthusiastic pentecostalists in Corinth that the gift of love was more important than the spiritual excitement of praying in tongues. Nevertheless, we can learn a great deal from the experience of the pentecostalists and the experience of the early Church. The atmosphere described by Luke is an extraordinary one that is very unlike the average church service in Britain today. A group of believers gathered together expectantly, possibly after days of fasting and preparation, looking to God to visit them with a power that would change their lives and direct them to his work and – BANG! – there was a great overflowing of spiritual and psychic enthusiasm that still reverberates through history. We could call it the big bang theory of the origins of Christianity. After that explosion at the Feast of Pentecost in Jerusalem, the Christian movement was driven throughout history; so unlike much contemporary Christian experience which is more like a soft plop than a loud bang.

I think there are two lessons we can learn from this story. One is that there is a streak of madness and extravagance in vital Christianity, and where it is missing what is left becomes thin, dull and lifeless. Christian history is full of stories of extravagant acts of love and self-sacrifice and spiritual experience. Our history is full of martyrs and mystics and great lovers of humanity. We should try to find a place in our own life for something of that unpredictable and exciting possibility.

Related to that expectation is the second lesson we can learn, and that is an acceptance and belief in the promise of Christ who told us in the Gospel of John that if we believed in him we would do the works that he did and greater works than these because he was going to the Father. Most of us trap ourselves in mediocrity because we don't believe in the power of God to rescue us from our own feebleness, either spiritual or moral. We don't expect great things to be done to us or through us. Yet here is Christ, the son of the living God, promising us that if we would only trust in him, believe his word, we would do greater works than he did, we would be set on fire with the spirit of Pentecost. Like you, I find it hard to believe this and I rarely trust the promise. My faith so often becomes a grim drudging thing, which I hold on to almost despite myself. Yet here I read a promise that tells me that if I will trust Christ he will set me on fire with his love, fill me with powers beyond my own powers and use me to do great works for his people.

That is why we have to hear again and again the great promise of Christ and look again and again at the experience of other Christians, both in our own time and in times long ago. Pentecost is a great day for dreaming dreams and seeing visions, both for ourselves and for our Church. I hope your dreams are big today. I hope your expectations are high. In the months before he was assassinated in 1968, Robert Kennedy went round the United States of America challenging his hearers to work for a better society and he always ended his speech with these words with which I'll end today:

> *Some men see things as they are and say why.*
> *I dream of things that never were*
> *and say 'Why not?'*

[Originally used at St Mary's Cathedral, Edinburgh 1990.]

Andrew

YOU will all, I am sure, appreciate the fact that I have been very busy since I became Bishop of Edinburgh – so busy, in fact, that I have been unable to find time to prepare a sermon for you this morning. Fortunately, a few nights ago I met a scholar while dining out in Edinburgh, which is really all that bishops do, and I confided my anxiety to him over a glass of port. Could he give me a new angle on the Apostle Andrew, since I had to say something about him to one of the most exacting and discerning audiences in Christendom?

'Funny you should mention that,' he said. 'In my research into sub-apostolic literature I have recently unearthed what is almost certainly Andrew's last letter, written from a prison cell in Achaia the night before he was executed. I'll give you my translation of the document and you can read it to your American friends. They'll enjoy the fact that it's a real scoop, the first reading in public of a unique find. Mind you, you'd better warn them that I've translated it rather freely.'

I thanked him profusely and borrowed his translation of the last Letter of Andrew the Apostle. Before I read it, let me give a brief introduction to it. First of all, it is almost certainly written to John the Apostle, living in Ephesus, on the coast of what is now Turkey. Andrew was writing from the governor's prison in Patras in Achaia, in South Western Greece. The mood of the letter is ruminative. Andrew is clearly looking into the past. In a series of flashbacks he summons up the memories of his extraordinary life. We must think of him sitting high up in the governor's prison, gazing out over the Gulf of Patras, watching the changing patterns of the wine red sea at sunset, remembering another sea in another land and one who stood on that seashore and called him to follow. After the usual felicitations to John, Andrew proceeds as follows:

* * *

'The governor is a kind man who clearly has no liking for this business. He allowed John Mark to stay with me most of the afternoon and he has given me permission to write this letter to you. Mark will deliver it to you at Ephesus. Strange to think that when you read it I shall have been dead for some weeks. I am not afraid to die tomorrow. The fact is that I am rather weary and feel it is time the Lord called me in to the shore to abandon my nets again and follow him. In spite of the momentous news Mark brought me, I have to confess that my old problem is still unresolved. I know it is foolish for an old man to be envious of his brother, especially after he is dead, but I have to admit that the old resentment is still there, and John Mark's news fanned it back to life. The awful thing is that it was not the fact that Simon Peter beat me in the race and went to the cross before me that brought back the old mixture of affectionate rivalry and real resentment; it was the way he insisted on dying that stirred the old exasperation into life. It was absolutely typical of Peter to insist on being crucified upside down. I know him so well: that turbulent mix of egotism and holiness, flamboyance and genuine humility. Peter was incapable of doing anything in moderation, and the way he chose to die is a fitting emblem of his whole life. The Lord often had to reprimand him for his exaggerated reactions, but we all knew that it was this very excess of energy he loved and chose to use, though sanctifying my brother was a long process. I have often meditated on the vast patience of the Lord Jesus for flawed and passionate people as long as he finds love in their hearts.

'The sun is beginning to sink, and the governor has very kindly brought me a light to write by. I shall stay awake tonight; little point in trying to sleep when I shall have rest enough tomorrow. The sea shifts constantly beneath my window, blood red for my last sunset. Ours was a quieter sea, its very storms, sudden and frightening though they were, were gentler than the constant anger that seems to strike these shores. I wonder if you ever recall those unbelievably distant days when we fished the Sea of Galilee, the sons of Zebedee and John. I can't remember much actual fishing, but I do remember the endless arguments, most of them prompted by Peter's outrageous views. I can recall your affectionate laughter when Peter would go into one of his harangues on the meaning of life and the exact nature of the kingdom that was to be inaugurated by the messiah. Even then Peter was convinced he'd be chief minister! What days they were, held in a kind of spell, like the strange silence before dawn. And then we were off into the desert after the Master's cousin, John the Baptiser. Peter was convinced he was the messiah, the one the whole earth longed for, but John claimed only to be preparing the way.

'Actually, I was the one who first met the Lord. The Baptist pointed him out to me and I remember being secretly delighted to have him to myself without my brother around to dominate the conversation. Mind you, that did not last for long, because I introduced Simon to the Lord as soon as I could. Even Simon was silent at that meeting – for a good thirty seconds! The Lord Jesus looked right through him, for all the world as if he were seeing his whole life, past and future, running before his eyes. Then he smiled – do you remember that smile, overwhelming because it was rare, totally without pretence, lighting up a countenance that was normally characterised by the tranquillity of profound sadness – anyway, he smiled at Simon and gave him the famous nickname: "Ah, so you are Simon: you'll be my rock from now on, Peter, the foundation-stone of my new temple." None of us knew what he meant, but we all felt something momentous had just happened, though the whole encounter could not have appeared less auspicious, with a few hens clucking round our feet as we sat under a straw sun shelter in someone's boat yard. As I say, even Simon was rendered silent for a few seconds before bursting into that torrent of language that often characterised him when embarrassed. I remember you and James telling me about some absolutely inane outburst on Mount Tabor when the Lord was transfigured before the three of you. Simon Peter never knew when to shut up, when to leave well alone, a fault that not infrequently characterises the spiritual leader. Amazing how the old resentments still smoulder! I've always been a bit hesitant in speech and slow in thought and jealous of Simon's unquenchable volubility.

'Anyway, that's how it all started; then there followed those three strange and exultant and tragic years. I can only describe them by saying we were in a permanent state of exalted ignorance. We knew somewhere inside ourselves who he was, yet somehow we didn't know, did not really connect it all together. It was all a bit like seeing a mountain through a swirling mist, catching the odd glimpse of the peak as the mist momentarily cleared. The moment I remember most vividly was that mysterious feeding of the five thousand. I suppose I remember it because I played a small part in it, but I am still baffled by it all. I can remember the panic that started to grip the inner circle of apostles with my brother, as usual, the spokesman. He was all for sending the mob away. They'd been following us for days, and one or two of us thought things might turn ugly: they always had such naive and primitive expectations of the Lord. He was always torn within himself as he watched them swarm round him: on the one hand you could sense the enormous compassion he felt, but there was a kind of sorrowing anger in him too, because their demands, their expectations were so straightforwardly material – who can blame the poor beggars. On that occasion the contrast between him and Simon Peter was obvious and characteristic: Simon got redder in the face and noisier by the minute; the Lord seemed to get paler, more still, deeper inside himself.

'I remember dragging a lad towards him because he had a few scraps of bread and fish wrapped up in a bit of old sail cloth. The boy had volunteered to share his frugal meal with those around him, and he tentatively thrust the grubby bundle at the Lord, whose face lit up at the selflessness of the gesture. I remember he put his arm round me, gave me the scraps from the boy and told me to share them round. Who can tell what happened next? I only remember doing what he said, and it was easy for me because it had always been my way.

'Much of what the Master said I did not understand, and I was always impatient with Peter and the rest when they argued with him. Not having much of a brain it was easier for me simply to do what he told me; even when I was puzzled by the order I did what I was told. "Do this," he would say, and I would, and something always happened. "Do this, do this in remembrance of me", that's something we have all learned to do, and thousands have fed on that word ever since, not knowing exactly what they did, but doing it because he bade it. "Do this," he said, "share it around", so I did and no one went away hungry. He never talked about what had happened. As always with him, he left it to us to make the connection, discover the meaning, read the riddle. In my naive way I decided there was very little mystery about it. The universe itself is an enormous mystery to me and I find it hard to comprehend how God could have called it into existence from nothing, but he did. The power and reality of God was present in the Master, the same creative power that made the universe worked in him. Could not the creative energy that set the stars in their courses and appointed the times and seasons of the earth have multiplied a few loaves and fishes? That's what I remember saying when we all got together afterwards to try to understand what happened. Thomas snorted at me in his impatient way, but no one came up with a better explanation and no one was able to dispute what had happened. You, beloved John, have always said that all reality has its origin in the thought or mind of God. I always recall you saying, "In the beginning was the word", and the word precedes the creative act. "Do this," he said, and I did it; the rest is history.

'My lamp is burning low, the oil almost used up, but it should be dawn soon, cock-crow. I am irresistibly reminded of his last dawn, of that other, awful cock-crow. I tremble with shame as I remember the thrill of malicious pleasure that ran through me when I heard of Peter's denials, wild intemperate denials, as bombastic as his proud claims of absolute commitment during that last supper. But none of us did well, except you, John, Mary the mother of the Lord, Mary of Magdala and a few other women. The rest of us fled in confusion, and I have often pondered the contrast between us. I suppose the difference was that you and the women who followed the Lord did not want anything from him; you just wanted to be with him, you worshipped him, though we would not then have used the word. I can see now, however, that most of the men who followed him wanted something from him: a place in his kingdom, to sit at his right hand at the great Independence Day banquet. How could we fail to be demoralised when it all started to run into the sand, when he went to that criminal's death, rather than into the palace of the king? The glory of his rising again on the third day has never totally expunged the memory of that weekend. But it is almost certain that in no other way could we have learned the lesson, the lesson that our values and expectations were totally at variance with his, that God's way to victory looks like defeat to the world. You saw this before any of us, showing us that the coronation, the anointing as king we had all planned on, happened on that hill outside Jerusalem, that his death was his glorification, defeat his victory. Hard lessons to understand, harder to live by and, yes, die for – my last test tomorrow.

'Cock-crow at last; just as my lamp splutters out, a silver band of light surges across the bottom of the eastern sky. So Paul is gone, too, beheaded, according to John Mark. He and my brother never really got on well together. Fitting that they should both die in Rome. Strange how we are all scattered over the face of the earth since that springtime in Galilee; stranger still how he is with all and each of us, no matter where we are, as I know he shall be with me later today. He goes with us to all our calvaries.

'I hear the guards stirring below. Soon they'll come for me. The governor has granted me a final favour, though he tried his best to dissuade me from it. He shook his head in amusement over my affectionate rivalry with Simon Peter, but he has agreed to allow me the final throw if not the last laugh. He has agreed to let me die on the *crux decussata*, the cross shaped like the Greek letter *chi:* not as dramatic as Simon's gesture, but I was always a less flamboyant person.

'O Simon, Simon how I miss your roar of a laugh, your head-long charge at life, your turbulent and unconquerable affection – be with me today.

'The tramp of feet on the stair. Farewell, beloved John. The peace of the Lord be with you.'

Andrew

* * *

I only want to add a footnote. We can, I think, judge that Andrew had the final laugh on his big brother. Nowhere is there a representation of the death of Peter, but Andrew's cross is recognised all over the world since it forms the central motif on the most famous flag in the world – the proud banner of Scotland.

[Originally used at the Church of the Advent, Boston.]

Alexander Heriot Mackonochie

CHRISTMAS Day in 1887 fell on a Sunday. Dr Oakley, the Dean of Manchester, began his sermon in the Cathedral with these words:

On Friday afternoon a long procession, chiefly of humble folk, went through the streets of London – I have regretted nothing so much for a long time as that I could not possibly be with them – to bury an unbeneficed clergyman, a clergyman with a history.

Alexander Mackonochie, who *was* the clergyman with a history, was a rather solid and stubborn Scot of the sort that make excellent engineers and keep carefully hidden the streak of wild poetry that lies in them, just like Kipling's chief engineer who saw 'predestination in the stride o' yon connecting rod'. He was last seen alive on a Thursday afternoon, December 15th 1887, while he was staying at Ballachulish with his friend the Bishop of Argyll. He did not return from a walk in the hills and his body was discovered two days later on the 17th by the Bishop who wrote: 'His body seemed almost frozen, and his head was half buried in the snow-wreath which had formed his last pillow.' He was buried a week later in London, on December 23rd.

Mackonochie became a priest in England during the second phase of the Oxford Movement and the times in which he ministered are best described by Henry Scott Holland:

There are few moments more dramatic in our Religious History than the recovery in the slums by the Oxford Movement of what it had lost in the University. How final that loss looked in Oxford itself can only be realised by those who have heard people like Edward King, of Lincoln, or Oakley, Dean of Manchester, tell of the dark days, when nothing remained of the Movement but the faint flickering flame on the altar at St Mary's which the loyalty of Charles Marriot still sustained in life. Pusey had been silenced. Newman had gone: and, in his going, had swept the place clean. The Heads of Colleges and the Dean were busy stamping out the last embers, by refusing Tutorships to known Tractarians, and by bullying the few Catholic Undergraduates who clung to Charles Marriot at St Mary's. They saw their triumph come. The Provost of Oriel, the President of St John's, the four Tutors, went about at large seeking whom they should devour. The cause was lost. So it seemed. When lo! It suddenly took on an entirely fresh lease of life. It made a new departure. It was to be heard of in all sorts of unexpected places. It wore unanticipated shapes, and spoke a different language. It had ceased to be Academic. It had become popular. It offered itself to every kind of novel opportunity and risk. It plunged into the dark places of our awful cities. It spent itself, with sacrificial ardour, in the service of the Poor. It shirked nothing: it feared nothing. It took blows and insults with a smile. It went ahead, in spite of menace and persecution. It spoke home to sinning souls and broken hearts, fast bound in misery and iron. It invaded the strongholds of Sin. It itself wore poverty as a cloak, and lived the life of the suffering and the destitute. It was irresistible in its elan, in its pluck, in its thoroughness, in its buoyancy, in its self-abandonment, in its laughter, in its devotion. Nothing could hold it. It won, in spite of all that could be done by Authorities in High Places, or by rabid Protestant Mobs, to drive it under.[1]

Mackonochie was one of the leaders of this second Spring of the Oxford Movement and he exemplified both aspects of its vision, which were to restore Catholic freedoms and traditions to Anglican worship and to bring the Gospel in all its richness, joy and tragedy to the poor. There were two points at issue in the first part of their programme and the debate that surrounded them eclipsed the real heart of their mission, which was to bring the faith back into what Scott Holland called 'the dark places of our awful cities'. The first point is rather technical and is the kind of thing that gets ecclesiastics a bad name. At issue was the status of the Ornaments Rubric of the First Prayer Book of Edward VI, which prescribed certain usages, including some that had fallen out of use and were re-introduced by the Oxford reformers. Were they still legal? In a robust editorial on the day of Mackonochie's funeral, the *Church Times*, which was then the house organ of the Catholic Movement, trumpeted:

> *No trained lawyer can doubt for a moment that the ritual law of the Church of England ever since 1662 has been the legality of all ornaments which were in use in the Church of England in the year 1548, before the First Prayer Book was issued. And even those who, to get over some polemical difficulties which the ruling presents, have substituted the 'First Prayer Book of Edward VI', for 'Second Year of Edward VI' in the reading of the Ornaments Rubric, acknowledge that all which was prescribed by that First Book continues lawful now. But that covers vestments and other litigated usages ....*[2]

But the issue was not just about the lawfulness of wearing vestments and mixing water with the wine in the chalice; it was more importantly about the freedom of the Church to order its worship without harassment from the State. That was the background to the ritualistic controversies that rocked the Church of England for generations. There were excesses on both sides and I have some sympathy with Mandell Creighton's weary riposte to a ritualistic curate from East London who unctuously reminded his Bishop that it was the clergy who, after all, had the cure of souls. 'Yes,' replied the Bishop, 'and like kippers you don't believe souls can be cured without smoke.'

Mackonochie was involved in these controversies, first at St George's in the East and then as first vicar of St Alban's Holborn, and he was the target of the Church Association's persecution in the courts. In 1868 the Privy Council decided against him on all the main issues of the suit brought by the Church Association, though the case was ostensibly brought by one of their stooges who had been smuggled on to the board of a school within the parish of St Alban's. Mackonochie, convinced that the court had no spiritual or even civil competence in the matter, simply ignored its decision and went on as before. While fresh measures were being prepared against him, Archbishop Tait persuaded him, for the peace of the Church, to exchange parishes with Father Suckling of St Peter's, London Docks, twenty years after his institution at St Alban's. But even this generous act of withdrawal did not satisfy the Church Association, which continued its pursuit of him through the courts. At last, broken down in health, he resigned the living and returned as a volunteer curate to his old parish. But his powers were broken and he became wandered and distracted at times. Presumably it was this vagueness that led to his losing his way in the forest of Mamore on December 15th 1887 and his death in the snow.

I have said that the leaders of the second phase of the Oxford Movement had a two-fold vision or fought on two fronts at the same time: for freedom in worship, on the one hand; and, related to it very closely, the bringing of the Gospel to the poor in the awful places of our cities, on the other. They won the first, less important, battle convincingly and transformed the public face of Anglican worship throughout the world. Bishop Francis Moncreiff once said to me that the best way to gauge the success of the Catholic Movement that sprang from Oxford in the nineteenth century was to look at the standard of Cathedral worship in England in the late twentieth century and compare it with what had gone before. They won that battle, all right, and their struggle had its martyrs; but we cannot say they won the second battle, the more important battle, the battle to win the poor for the Church, so that it may not only be a Church for the poor, but a Church of the poor. Our generation tends to see that battle in political terms, and we must never shrink from the political implications of the Gospel, but men like Mackonochie and Stanton in London, or Laurie in Edinburgh and the McBain brothers in Glasgow, saw it in more personal terms. For them the priestly call was a call to holiness and one of the classic forms of Christian sanctity is identification with the poor.

Catholic social action has always had two roots. The first is the Doctrine of the Incarnation. If you are ever asked 'why do Anglo-Catholics, like blondes, have more fun?', the answer is 'because they believe in the Incarnation'. They love the world and all its beauty and perplexity, because they see it as a sacrament of the unutterable beauty of God. Beneath all the nonsense and traipsing about there is a glorious truth concealed: 'The world is charged with the grandeur of God,' in Hopkins' great words. 'The Holy Ghost over the bent world broods with warm breast and with ah! bright wings.' So the Mackonochies and the Stantons and the Lauries and the McBains, their soutanes flapping round their ankles, went in search of the incarnate Christ through the bliss and heartache of their great ministry to the poor. And how they laughed as they battled! Most of them were well-connected, so they brought their cousins in from the West End to help at the settlements and fresh-air camps they ran. And gradually the word went through the land and broke through the social determinism of the times, and reform came, because workers organised and a generation was at last taught to listen, however slowly, to their claims. Most of those priests were pragmatists, fighting for improvement, amelioration – but some went further. They were captured by the haunting and perplexing vision of a whole society redeemed, not just individuals within it. They longed and planned for the day when the kingdoms of this world would be the kingdom of our God and of his Christ. So they created what they called a sociology, an attempt to tackle the problems of systemic, not just individual evil. They turned their thoughts to the ethics of institutions as well as persons. Some of them became fully-blown Utopians, like Conrad Noel, whose Red Flag still hangs in Thaxted Church. So the doctrine of the Incarnation led them to the dispossessed and it filled some of them with visions of a transformed society, become God's kingdom on earth.

The second root of Catholic social action is a mystical identification with the poor. Those slum priests of the Catholic Movement loved the poor. They didn't use them or recruit them, they *loved* them. They were there long before the prim young Fabian social workers descended in their droves. (I am reminded of the woman from East London who said of these earnest young puritans: 'Ooh, I do 'ate being worked among.') There was a Franciscan quality about the men and women who gave themselves to the work, and they created a climate which led to the revival of the Franciscan Order in the Anglican Communion and several other communities committed to the pursuit of holy poverty. Much of it was the hidden work of identification with the poor. It is impossible to compute the impact or effectiveness of so many secret acts of surrender. Who can tell what redemptive energy was released into the great struggle between light and darkness by the mere fact that generations of London urchins called a curate at St Albans 'Dad' and turned out in their tens of thousands to mourn his death in March 1913. Romantic? Oh, yes. Filled with the same romance as the eternal gospel of a heartbroken God who goes forth from himself in search of his children. Oh, yes, it was romantic, all right, as romantic as the great prologue of John.

It seems to me that the Church today needs to rekindle that romantic vision and that the Catholic Movement, in particular, needs to recapture it. We need to recover two things today, holiness and laughter, both for their own sake and because they commend the Gospel to others and especially to the poor. The way to honour Alexander Mackonochie, then, is not by remembering him dead in the snows of Argyll or by recalling the triumph of the Catholic party in its battles over ritual, but by recapturing something of the vision glorious that led him and many others into the bleak places of our nation to claim them for Christ.

[Originally used at St Brides, Onich 1987.]

1   Henry Scott Holland: *A Bundle of Memories* (Wells, Gardner, Darton & Co).
2   *Church Times*, 23rd December 1887.

Isabella

The Lord whom ye seek, shall suddenly come to his temple.
~ Malachi 3:1 ~

I WONDER if you've come across the novels of Barbara Pym? She died a few years ago, but since her death there has been something of a revival of interest in the half dozen or so novels she wrote. Nothing as vulgar as bestsellerdom, of course. Barbara is for the discriminating palate: very white and dry, leaving an aftertaste that is at once wistful and astringent. Nothing very much appears to happen in her books. There is little drama or excitement. Instead, by an accumulation of small details she paints a picture of the extraordinary heroism and strength of very ordinary lives. Or, to change the metaphor, it's as though she had decided to find the strong heart of society. It is the heart, after all, that keeps the body functioning. It's hidden away in secret, but it is what makes the rest work. Barbara Pym disdains the flashy external type of behaviour. She focuses, instead, on secret people, hidden away in small villages or unfashionable suburbs where, we are led to feel, something profoundly important is going on, something that somehow redeems the rest of us. Her main characters are usually unmarried, well-educated, vaguely middle-aged, or sometimes elderly Anglo-Catholic women. It is a group I know well. They are the secret elect of God, the heart of the Church, the reason why, I often think, God has not rained fire and brimstone down upon the rest of us this while past.

One of my heroines was such a person. Her name was Isabella. She was a secretary in a law office in Edinburgh, a job which she fulfilled with steely efficiency. There was a strong East coast reserve in Isabella, which made her shy and a little chilly. In Auden's phrase, her's was distinctly a private face in public places. She would never have done in California. She lived in rooms all her life and her nearest living relative, when I knew her, was a distant cousin. But Isabella had an intense inner life. She loved the Church. For years she was senior sacristan at Old St Paul's, and she stuck tenaciously to a powerful and disciplined spirituality throughout her life. She went on retreat twice a year to several dearly loved convents. Once a year she made a pilgrimage to the shrine of our Lady of Walsingham. Every morning she said her intercessions, and in the evening she prayed. She used to pray in the morning, but something started happening that made it necessary for her to move her prayer time to the evening. I have known only a few people in my life who have achieved the prayer of mystical union with Christ. You read of this kind of prayer in mystical literature. In it the soul is released from the person in an indefinable way and has intense communion with Christ. When that state is entered into, it can last for hours, during which the subject is oblivious to their surroundings. St Theresa of Avila was a person who had achieved this state, almost to the point of embarrassment. She had to chain herself to the railings in the chapel to prevent herself levitating to the ceiling, so rapt was her experience of the presence of Christ. Well, Isabella had achieved this state. Diffidently, she tried to explain to me what had started happening, as though I could help her. Compared to her, of course, I was in the spiritual kindergarten. There were probably no more than a handful of people in Scotland who had this gift of prayer. I can remember the moment when I realised that Isabella was probably one of the most significant Christian forces in the country, yet hardly anyone knew her! She never went to public meetings. She was almost unknown to other members of Old St Paul's, yet I came increasingly to realise that, as God saw these things, she, and not the public Christians who were known, was the heart of the Christian cause in Scotland.

She died a rather uncomfortable death, unable to speak because they had to give her a tracheotomy and feed her by bypassing her throat. I remember her last summer. How we missed seeing her erect figure in the Lady Chapel where she came to early mass several days a week. I remember once towards the end describing how I'd just come from celebrating mass in the Lady Chapel. We both sat there with tears streaming down our faces as I described how everything was looking and how she was still close to that beloved altar. She died shortly after that, brave and uncomplaining, her eyes fixed on the invisible presence of Jesus.

I was her executor and inherited all her prayer books. Those of you who remember the golden days of the Anglo-Catholic movement will recognise the kind of thing I found. The *English Missal*, with a black elastic band round it. The *Missal* itself full of prayer cards: 'I prayed for you today at the shrine of our Lady of Walsingham, Constance: June 1960.' Ordination cards and first mass cards from every priest she had ever known; and she had scolded and loved generations of curates at Old St Paul's. Post cards of English convents. An olive leaf from the Holy Land. And there were other prayer books: The *Centenary Prayer Book*, published in 1933 to mark the hundredth anniversary of the start of the Oxford Movement; the *St Andrew's Roman Catholic Missal,* produced by Belgian Benedictines (like many of us, Isabella, loyal Anglican that she was, had always loved the great Roman Church); and piles of notebooks of her own meditations, and full notes of almost every retreat she had made since the 1920s, including six that I had conducted during her last years. Strange to see one's own stumbling affirmations lovingly preserved in spidery handwriting on someone else's cheap notebooks. I've kept them all. They are a powerful sacramental force for me. Sometimes I sit with them on my lap and finger through them, conscious that they represent the struggle of a whole lifetime with prayer and the precious, yet elusive, presence of the supernatural Christ; and something of her relationship with Jesus comes through this pile of dog-eared notebooks and well-thumbed prayer manuals. Hers, you see, was a life of magnificent, if silent, spiritual triumph. Away from all the movements that had caused upheaval in the Church, all the debate and change that had characterised the times, all the strutting and posing and raised voices and angry faces of the day, she had won the real victory – and no one knew about it, except God. He had come to her during many a lonely vigil in a small room in an Edinburgh back street. One day, when we see history from God's perspective, Isabella Crockett will be shown to have been one of the most important people of the twentieth century, and we'll know then what her prayer wrought.

But this should not surprise us, for it has been ever thus. When the Lord whom we seek suddenly comes to his temple, it is always with stealth to the quiet ones who wait. The redemption of Israel came, not to the anointed priests of the temple, nor to the learned and ostentatious scribes of the law, but to an old man and woman of prayer who waited in the shadows for the consolation of Israel. Only Simeon and Anna were there when Mary and Joseph brought Jesus to the temple. Only they saw the salvation of God. It is God's way forever. He puts down the mighty from their seat and exalts the humble and meek. But only his eyes see that exaltation. Only he knows the souls that redeem the rest of us by the longing and passion of their praying. The Church is not saved by the windy rhetoric of its official exponents, but by the silent prayer of its secret saints in all the backstreets of the world – unknown to us, but known intimately to God. When John Keble despaired of the salvation of the Church of England, he took himself deep into the countryside and prayed and ministered to a village congregation. And from that hidden vicarage there streamed forth an invisible spiritual power that transformed the Anglican Communion.

That is still the way he cleanses and renews his Church. He comes back to it suddenly and in secret, and cleanses it by the prayer of his unknown saints. Several conclusions can be drawn from this. Whatever is the world's way, the renewal and purification of the Church comes only upon the recovery of real spiritual seriousness among its members. Cardinal Newman used to say of his experience of the clergy and their impact upon people, that intellect made the most difference in the short run, but sanctity made the most difference in the long run. It is holiness, not cleverness that really converts, because a person's cleverness can be a purely human force, while sanctity is full of the presence of God. Anyone who knows anything about the history of the great parishes of the Anglican Communion knows this is true. Back there in the past there was once a saintly rector whose influence is felt long after the clever words of his more brilliant successors have been forgotten. On the whole, clergy are a useless and expensive encumbrance upon the people of God, unless they are trying, in the secret struggles of prayer, to let God purify their lives.

But that must not be my last word. I have entered it for my own and other clergy's sake, because of the great danger in which our vocation places us. But this is not a day for us. It is a day which reminds us of the redemptive role of the private people, the saints of God's heart who wait upon his glory in secret vigil, and are known to him alone – Mary and Joseph; Simeon and Anna; Isabella and Edward; John and Betty. Unknown people from all the back streets of history, obscure and unregarded – except in heaven, where it is known how their faithfulness, somehow, redeems the rest of us.

[Originally used at the Church of the Advent, Boston, 1982.]

Cuthbert

You, therefore, must be perfect, as your heavenly Father is perfect.
~ Matthew 5:48 ~

WHEN I was young and pious – and I am afraid that now I am neither – part of my Lent reading used to be hagiography, writings about the saints. I had a little book that gave a saint for every day and I would dutifully read the portion appointed. I have to confess that the kind of thing I read then would bring tears of laughter and disbelief to my eyes today, but in those days I read it with great seriousness. Those of you who are familiar with this sub-species of literature will recognise the kind of thing I came across. There would be a bare outline of the saint's life, an account of the miracles he wrought, the date of his death and a list of the objects for which his prayers were reckoned to be particularly efficacious. Here's a fabricated example of the kind of thing I read:

St Prigissimus, born in Gaul in 517 to devout parents, was noted for his piety at an early age. At the age of five he insisted on sewing thorns into his undershirt in order to identify with his Lord's passion and death. His first miracle was performed when he was seven upon his uncle, who was a coarse and licentious man, much afflicted with stones in the kidney: upon receiving a godly admonishment from his saintly nephew he spontaneously emitted the stones at the young man's feet, to the praise and wonder of the onlookers. When he was nine years old Prigissimus refused henceforth to look at any member of the female sex, including his own mother and sisters.

Thereafter, whenever he encountered a female, he pulled his hood over his face and looked down upon the earth, in order to preserve his purity. At eleven he miraculously struck two of his school-fellows dumb for blasphemously mocking him. He entered the Monastery of the Great Yawn on his thirteenth birthday and was made abbot when he was 17. He lived on turnips till he was 32, when he died in great agony, though without complaint. He was canonised in 595 and is the patron of those who suffer from gall and kidney stones, for the removal of which his prayers are powerfully efficacious. His emblem is the turnip and his day of commemoration is February 30th.

I realise now, of course, that books of that sort were the religious equivalent of Dan Dare and Superman comics. When we are young we nurse fantasies about magic deliverances and super-human powers, we long for some secret formula that will remove us from the common rut of human nature and endow us with effortless abilities. We want results without having to work for them, sanctity without tears, heroism without struggle.

But as the clock moves on we realise that life is not like that, so these magic figures from comic books and Christian legend have nothing to teach us. At this stage we need heroes we can identify with. We are still forming ourselves, still full of hope about the greatness that awaits us after we have disciplined ourselves, overcome our weaknesses and built upon our strengths. We still believe that we can overcome our frailties, so now we want stories about people like ourselves who battled against weakness and were made strong. We are comforted by the fact that St Augustine was dissolute in his youth and St Paul was a persecutor. If they could get over it, so can we. But the clock keeps moving and one day we realise that there has been no improvement in our lives, no great change, no increase in sanctity or self-control, no great achievement. In fact, we are very ordinary: ordinarily lazy; ordinarily lustful; ordinarily greedy; and like every other ordinary person, we have long since lost any spiritual ambition to be perfect, to be complete and rounded and fulfilled, the finished version of the very unfinished person we are.

72

At this stage we probably stop reading about saints and heroes altogether, because they only make us feel awful, make us feel like losers. Of course, we cannot altogether avoid encounter with heroic individuals, with people better than we are, either in history or among people we know, so either of two reactions can start to build in us. The first is a sort of quiet despair about ourselves. We feel that there will never be improvement in our lives: *that* bad habit will never be given up and *that* virtue will never be acquired. We'll go to God empty-handed, with nothing made of our lives at all, though we realise now that all that would have been required back there was a little more self-control, a tiny bit of extra endurance, but now it is too late. Despair of this sort is a spiritual killer, but it can become a friend if we turn it into a sort of rueful humility, a realism about ourselves. If we face the truth about ourselves, honestly, even humorously, we create the conditions in which the spark of spiritual longing can kindle in us again, bringing a mid-winter Spring and a second growth, because it is never too late to start growing.

Years ago I took down in my notebook some words from Geoffrey Faber's biography of Benjamin Jowitt. I liked them then, but now I can really feel their force. He wrote about Jowitt as he got older: 'The great, the tragic difference between youth and old age – how youth can form the character of old age, but does not realise its opportunity, how age knows only too clearly what youth should have done but can no longer do it equally. The saving adverb "equally" is a word to notice,' continues Faber. 'The door is not closed till the very end of life.' [1]

The other reaction is much graver and more common. This is when we descend into cynicism. Cynicism is a kind of envy, a kind of hatred of another's goodness, that leads us to debunk the achievements of people better than ourselves, to pour scorn upon their virtues. Ours is a cynical age, an age without heroes or ideals. That is why our muck-raking press loves to dig up dirt about our leaders and celebrities, likes to parade their flaws and frailties before our envious eyes. It all serves to confirm us in our own ordinariness and weakness, and offers us a bitter sort of comfort for our own failures.

That is why we need to go on thinking about the saints and heroes. We need them because they remind us that human nature can be perfected by grace and the generous surrender of our wills to God, and that we must never settle despairingly or cynically into a passive acceptance of our weakness. It is God's will for us that we should grow into our full stature, move towards the fulfilment of that character which is our destiny, our perfection. Affectionate remembrance of the saints and heroes, the Cuthberts and Columbas and the whole company of heaven, will nerve us to continue the race that is set before us. I think that Cuthbert, in particular, can teach us many things and I offer two of them briefly for your meditation.

Cuthbert often went on visitations to remote villages to preach the Gospel to them. *Bede* tells us that Cuthbert 'often remained a week, sometimes two or three, nay, even a whole month, without returning home; but dwelling among the mountains, taught the poor people, both by the words of his preaching and also by his own holy conduct'. Cuthbert was an evangelist and teacher who helped the cause of the Gospel to grow in our land. That cause is under threat today, and the Church he helped to establish seems to shrink inexorably both in size and influence. Inspired by Cuthbert, we must learn again how to commend the Gospel to the people of our day, both by our preaching and by our holy living. A mysterious missionary paralysis afflicts the Church of our time. We seem to have lost confidence in the message we are sent to proclaim. Cuthbert's example should re-kindle our zeal for the Gospel, the true Gospel – not the scolding, carping, accusatory type of Christianity that makes the average person run a mile, but the bold joy of the Gospel of God's unconditional love for us all.

Cuthbert was an evangelist, but he was also a man of prayer, a solitary, a hermit, going off to the Island of Farne where he died a solitary death in 687. He endured as seeing him who is invisible. He was caught by the beauty and mystery of God and people saw God's glory reflected in his countenance. People will catch the glow of the Gospel from us if we ourselves are touched by it, kindled into flame by a coal from the altar of the Holy of Holies. Like Cuthbert and all the saints of God, we must learn to turn our eyes towards the invisible, towards the secret mystery of God, which fills the universe, yet is known in the depths of our own heart. To that God be glory and worship, for time and for eternity, throughout all ages, world without end. Amen.

[Originally used at the 1300th Anniversary, Bamburgh, June 1987.]

1   Geoffrey Faber: *Jowitt* (Faber & Faber: London).

All Saints

Jesus was at Bethany, in the house of Simon the leper. As he sat at table, a woman came in carrying a bottle of very costly perfume, pure oil of nard. She broke it open and poured the oil over his head. Some of those present said indignantly to one another, 'Why this waste? The perfume might have been sold for more than three hundred denarii and the money given to the poor'; and they began to scold her. But Jesus said, 'Leave her alone. Why make trouble for her? It is a fine thing she has done for me. You have the poor among you always, and you can help them whenever you like; but you will not always have me. She has done what lay in her power; she has anointed my body in anticipation of my burial. Truly I tell you: wherever the Gospel is proclaimed throughout the world, what she has done will be told as her memorial.'

~ Mark 14:3-9 *(Revised English Bible)* ~

IT is easy to understand why they reproached her, why they felt the way they did. After all, three hundred denarii was a whole year's pay for a labourer in those days, a lot of money to pour over anyone's head. And anyway, the gesture was overdone. It was tasteless, precisely the sort of extravagant and operatic gesture you'd expect from a woman like her. Why did the master encourage these extraordinary people to hang around him? Few of them had ever done an honest day's work in their lives, though they always seemed to have plenty of money to splash around. Yes, it's easy to understand their indignation: 'Why *was* the perfume thus wasted?'

There are always plenty of people around who'll take this line of scrupulous fiscal responsibility. I remember years ago in Glasgow, long before it became the City of Culture, a group applied to the town council for a grant to bring a famous ballet company to the city. The application was rejected and the convener of the relevant committee told the press: 'Whit this toon needs is *bathrooms,* no belly dancers.'

You get the same response every time an appeal is launched to restore a cathedral or a historic parish church – it is said, of course, that we'll never ever again *build* another cathedral; those monuments to the extravagance of faith are forever a thing of the past. On all sides we hear: 'Why *was* the perfume thus wasted? For this perfume might have been sold for more than three hundred denarii and the money given to the poor.' It is difficult to come up with a strictly logical answer, because there is no doubt that the money could always be spent on other, more urgent things. The poor *are* always with us and their needs are limitless. Why *is* the perfume thus wasted?

People who ask this question are usually worthy and serious. They have heard the summons of God to feed the poor, count the cost, be sober and upright, wise stewards of their master's goods. They like to plan and calculate and work everything out without frivolity. They cast long looks at unnecessary flourishes. They see life as unremittingly earnest and serious. The issues that confront them are too urgent to be trifled with, so they buckle themselves to God's tasks with unflagging grimness. They are spiritual monetarists, ever on the lookout for waste and extravagance, and their cry is ever the same: 'Why *was* the perfume thus wasted?'

Their tragedy is that they have missed out a whole dimension in their calculations, a whole dimension of creation and a whole dimension of God. God *is* the God of the desert and its frugality; he is the God of the wise steward who manages his household in due season; he is the God of the wise builder who sits down and counts the cost before digging the foundations. Yes, he is all of these; but he is something much more. He is also God of the dance, God of the feast, God of play, inspirer of poets and musicians, artist of creation, the mad genius who painted the vast canvas of the sky. Think of the sheer prodigal waste of creation. Listen to some words from an American poet:

Is it not by his high superfluousness we know
Our God? For to equal a need
Is natural, animal, mineral: but to fling
Rainbows over the rain,
And beauty above the moon, and secret rainbows
On the domes of deep sea-shells,
And make the necessary embrace of breeding
Beautiful also as fire.
Not even the weeds to multiply without blossom
Nor the birds without music ....
The extravagant kindness of God.[1]

The impulse to celebrate life by art and music and extravagant gestures of devotion is part of our very likeness to God who set the stars in their courses at the foundation of the world and all the children of God shouted for joy. That is why we have created buildings like this, reckless in their extravagant beauty, poured out in uncalculating love to God.

And something of this God-like extravagance is found in the lives of the saints. But behind the saints stands Jesus, the King of Saints; he is the source and inspiration of their heedless devotion. I shiver when I think of Jesus Christ and the intensity of his life. There was a divine recklessness in him, a refusal to calculate the odds. One feels in his presence an absolute generosity and courage. And it's infectious. It catches people and changes and enlarges them. The saints in particular are those who have been formed into some pattern of his likeness. If we consider the nature of Jesus Christ, the pattern of Christian holiness, we will find it repeated down the ages even to this very day.

For instance, think of the sorrowful anger of Christ, that anger which is the passionate aspect of love. And think of all the saints who have raged against the dying of the light in humanity. I mention only one – General Booth, the founder of the Salvation Army. Think of the anger of love that sent him and his soldiers into all the dark places of the earth where God's children are tormented and deprived. And you will find him and his followers to this day, working selflessly on the other side of the tracks, down in the abyss. Do you know that it was the Salvation Army that closed Devil's Island, the dreaded penal colony of France in the West Indies? It was the anger of Christ working in that remarkable man which stamped out that and many other evils. I cannot resist quoting Vachell Lindsay's great poem about General Booth entering heaven:

Booth died blind and still by faith he trod,
Eyes still dazzled by the ways of God.
Booth led boldly, and he looked the chief
Eagle countenance in sharp relief,
Beard a-flying, air of high command
Unabated in that holy land.

Jesus came from out the court-house door,
Stretched his hands above the passing poor.
Booth saw not, but led his queer ones there
Round and round the mighty court-house square.
Then, in an instant all that blear review
Marched on spotless, clad in raiment new.
The lame were straightened, withered limbs uncurled
And blind eyes opened on a new, sweet world.

And when Booth halted by the curb for prayer
He saw his Master through the flag-filled air.
Christ came gently with a robe and crown
For Booth the soldier, while the throng knelt down.
He saw King Jesus. They were face to face.
And he knelt a-weeping in that holy Place.[2]

And think of the enormous gentleness of Christ, his love for children, the broken, the sinful, the despised. How often that pattern is repeated in the saints. Think of the poor man of Assisi, St Francis. Think of his love for all the little ones, his care for lepers, his poetry and joy, his incredible self-denial. Chesterton says that when St Francis died lying on the bare, hard ground in the snow, 'the stars which passed above him had for once, in all their shining cycles round the world of labouring humanity, looked down upon a happy man'.[3]

But think also about the gentleness of Christ today as he responds through his saints to HIV and its desolating impact. AIDS has brought out the worst in Christians, but it has also brought out the best. There are hundreds of saints in this city tonight hard at work, visiting, bathing, touching, clothing God's little ones.

And think of the sheer intellectual power of Christ. We often forget this aspect of Christ's nature, seeing him as a simple folk-singing country boy, rather than as the man whose moral and intellectual stature put the pharisees to flight and confounded the doctors of the law. Think of the great treasures of Christian thought which have flowed from that source. In every age since his resurrection many of the greatest intellects of their day have been put at his service, and still are. The Christian Church is not, and never has been, an intellectually underprivileged group of mindless rhapsodists. This century has not been short of men and women of formidable mental power and originality, who have used it to search the deep things of God and set forth his ways before the people of their day. If it's intellectual stimulation you want, then you'd better enroll in the Communion of Saints straight away.

We sometimes think of Jesus as a sort of dreamy and distracted figure who went about in a heavenly swoon. Far from it. He was a leader and an organiser of genius. He may not have had a word processor and fax machine, but he knew how to administer, how to make use of men and women, how to send them out to work, how to train them, how to organise the masses. Whatever else it was, the Feeding of the Five Thousand was a brilliant piece of organisation.

And his servants have been at it ever since: they organised education and medical services throughout the world before any government tackled them, and there's a fair amount of evidence which suggests that they made just as good a job of it. And they are still at it, sweeping back the tide of human misery with patient unselfregarding toil. Think of the eons of time spent patiently listening, think of the tons of corn administered, the gallons of soup poured out, the wait by the bedside, the patient teaching of disordered and disturbed children. Think of the millennia of hours spent in just caring for people, when the Jordan was swelling and darkness lay all around. Much, much has been left undone, but no age has been without its witnesses who have patiently administered love after the manner of the fashion of Jesus Christ. O, all ye doctors and nurses, bless ye the Lord: O, all ye teachers, and social workers, bless ye the Lord: O, all ye organisers and despised bureaucrats, bless ye the Lord – praise him and magnify him for ever. The organising love of Christ.

Finally, think of the prayer life of Jesus, his going apart constantly to pray, his communion with the Father, his waiting upon God. And think of all the great men and women of prayer in the Christian Church. What an incredible company the great mystics are! You find them in every Christian tradition, but above all in the great Roman Catholic Church with its unbroken history of spiritual formation and discipline, holding before us the beacon light of unceasing prayer as the foundation of all holiness.

But our own Church is not without its great witnesses. I think, for instance, of Evelyn Underhill. Like many catholic-minded Anglicans, all her life she was drawn to the great Roman Church, though she remained a committed Anglican. She said of the Anglican Church that she was quite content to remain within it because, while it might not be the city of God, it was certainly a respectable suburb thereof!

On the eve of All Saints Day in 1919, Baron von Hugel wrote to his niece Gwen: 'Gwen, look up with me tomorrow! Oh, what a glorious, touching company.'[4] What a glorious, touching company indeed – the Communion of Saints. The Church is not just us. It is not just all living Christians. It is all Christians who ever were. We are members of the most interesting family the world has ever known. And they are with us today in this lovely place as we celebrate their festival. And what they suggest to me is holy recklessness, a joyous, uncalculating generosity of spirit that pours itself out in devotion. Wouldn't it be marvellous if our Church could be caught up by that spirit? Instead of being defensive and insecure, parading the ramparts anxiously, on the lookout for enemies, keeping guard on the perfume of the Gospel – wouldn't it be wonderful if it knocked all the walls down and marched out into the open, laughing and eager to serve and embrace the world for which Christ died? This Church in its polychromatic exuberance always suggests to me that kind of generosity of spirit.

Let us then use the inspiration of this day to recall us all to the recklessness of the Gospel. Let us nerve ourselves to pour the perfume out, not keep it to ourselves, in the name of the Church's Lord who emptied himself for our sake and who now lives and reigns with the Father and the Holy Spirit, one God, for ever and ever. Amen.

[Originally used at All Saints, Margaret Street, London, November 1990.]

1   Robinson Jeffers: *Be Angry at the Sun* (Random House: New York).
2   Vachell Lindsay: *Collected Works.*
3   From his small essay on St Francis.
4   Baron Von Hugel: *Letters to a Niece* (J M Dent: London).

Mary

SOME years ago I saw a comic strip that was meant to illustrate the role of Our Lady in the work of salvation. It showed a very high tower, fortified and tight shut, the drawbridge pulled up. The tower represented heaven. At the foot of the tower, by the great door, stood a group of men and women begging to be let in. They were imploring God the Father, God the Son and God the Holy Spirit, who were seen on the top of the tower gazing over the landscape, ignoring the pleas of the people shut out below. But round the back something else was going on: at a window, high up in the tower, sat Our Lady, dangling a gigantic rosary down to the ground. Up it were scrambling men, women and children, who had turned from the anger of God to the kindness of Mary and were cheerfully clambering into heaven through the back window.

Now that is bad theology and no Church would accept it. It puts a wedge between Mary and God and suggests that Mary is more approachable than God, more tolerant and indulgent; the kind of mother we all run to when the anger of the father puts fear into our hearts. Well, bad theology it may be, but it is very interesting psychology and it corresponds to a real tension in the Christian understanding of God and even in the Christian experience of God. We find in Christian theology and in Christian experience a tension between the God who judges our sins and the God who has mercy on the weakness that leads us to sin. We find in the biblical picture of God a stern father who angrily denounces our wickedness and constantly calls us to perfection; but we also find a picture of him as a loving husband who forgives his wife's adultery, a nurse who cherishes her children, a hen who gathers her chickens under her wings. In fact, we find in God condemnation and consolation; judgement and mercy. And this tension, this mysterious contrast in the biblical picture of God and in the human experience of God, corresponds to something in our nature.

We are at the same time morally and spiritually lazy, yet filled with longings for goodness and holiness. There is something in us, in Hopkins' phrase, that 'wants war, wants wounds', wants to be surrendered and dedicated to something great and holy. And that holy ambition in our hearts exactly corresponds to the great call of God. The God of the Bible calls us to two things: personal holiness and the struggle for social justice, the care of our own souls and a passionate care for the poor and the needy. That is the great double imperative that burns through the pages of scripture: 'Be thou holy' and 'Inasmuch as you did not do it unto the least of these you did not do it unto me.'

There is something in us that answers to the great summons of God to personal perfection and unself-regarding service of the needy. But our own heaviness and weakness pull us back again and again, so God's great call to us to dedicate ourselves begins to sound like a reproach, begins to feel in our hearts like judgement and ends by convicting us of sin, ends by condemning us because, in spite of many resolutions and enthusiastic efforts, we have not become holy, have made little progress, may even have gone backwards, lost our ideals, lost any expectation that we can grow. And what is true in the personal sphere is doubly true in our public record of care for the needy. We have grown more comfortable and the cry of the needy that used to sound so painfully in our ears is hardly heard at all now. They are well away from where we live and after a while it is possible to forget that they even exist.

Yet that voice continues to cry out in the wilderness of scripture, only now we do not hear it with excitement; we hear it with increasing discomfort, even dread. We did try, we wanted to be holy – but self-pleasing is so insidious and powerful and it has taken us over and now we are locked into it, though we still hear that voice crying,

crying in the wilderness, so that it torments us with a sense of loss and failure. And this is compounded by the impotence we feel in the face of poverty and human misery. We begin to suspect that our comfort is built somehow on their discomfort, that by their wounds we prosper. But we are afraid to disturb our own security, so we won't even look at measures that might help, because we might have to pay for them, deprive ourselves, share. The poor are always going to be with us, we hear Jesus say, and we also know that he cares passionately for the poor, loves the poor and calls us to share their poverty; so that's another thing we can't hear, another way in which the voice of God in scripture begins to sound like judgement, begins to hurt us where once it excited us.

So that comic strip begins to make sense. One side of our experience of God is judging us, hurting us. Like the bridesmaids who brought no oil for their lamps and were locked out of the wedding feast, we feel that God is locking us out because we have disappointed him. Anyone who listens to scripture with its exalted challenges and demands is bound to feel this kind of defeat, this sense of something we long for that is beyond our grasp. But we are rescued from despair by another note that sounds in scripture, a note that is falsely but significantly illustrated in that comic strip. This is the loving-kindness of God, the understanding of God, the divine gentleness that knows our weaknesses and accepts them. It is, in fact, the motherliness of God, that sense of total acceptance of us, just as we are. There is something in all of us that always needs to be mothered in that sense. This mothering is the complete opposite of judging. It is not conditioned upon anything except the kindness and yearning towards you of the mother.

I had a very concrete experience of this from my own mother that has remained with me for about 50 years. Most of the boys of my generation, brought up in the West of Scotland during the Second World War, were great fans of the cinema. It was our magic palace, the source of many of our symbols, the place we escaped to from the poverty of our surroundings. I remember we used to take the *Sunday Mail* and there was a whole page devoted to advertising the pictures that were on in Glasgow, 20 miles away from where I lived. I can remember the names of the picture houses still, though many of them are closed now: The Gaumont, Sauchiehall Street; The Regal, Renfield Street; The Roxy, The La Scala, The Rialto, and so on. On Sundays, then, imagine me pouring over the advertisements for the films showing in these faraway palaces of dreams. One Monday morning I found myself telling a group of my friends during the break that I'd been to one of these films and I made up a story that seemed to fit the exciting things I had read about the film in the paper the day before. Soon I was locked into a fantasy: every Monday morning a group of boys would gather round me and ask me what film I'd seen and I'd spin them a story, based on a few lines from the *Sunday Mail*. And I also began to feel guilty about what I was doing: guilty, but locked into something I could see no way out of. I can remember one night I lay for hours in an agony of guilt about what I was doing and finally I crept through to my mother and tearfully poured out the story. And what I received was absolute consolation, absolute mothering: no condemnation, no scolding. I can remember her very words: 'It's all right, Dick,' she said, 'you just have a good imagination.' And I was released. I was understood. I stopped pretending on Monday mornings and just told stories, but an enormous burden was lifted from me, without a word of judgement: I was truly mothered.

And we find that mothering in God, in scripture: that sense that we are understood in all our failure and utterly accepted. That whole strand of scripture is imaged in Our Lady, who doesn't say much at all: she is there, a tender presence, balancing all the masculine harshness that seems to pour out of the Judean desert. And around that image of Our Lady, that image of the mothering we find in God, the nursing, nurturing aspect of God, there is a cluster of lovely words: meekness, gentleness, humbleness – words that draw us through our tears, words we can hear through all our failures; and if we hear them really deep in our hearts a strange thing happens. We still stand convicted of failure and we are still wounded by that conviction, but at the very same time we feel utterly accepted and understood, and a great and healing contradiction takes place within us: this God who calls us to holiness and the struggle for righteousness is also the one who understands our frailty and who offers us healing and acceptance. So the total Christian experience, as well as official Christian doctrine, becomes a great, yet healing paradox: we are judged, yet forgiven; sinners, yet justified; failures, who make it through. On this day we should open ourselves to both aspects, both ends of the great Christian paradox. We should hear again the great and wounding call to holiness and absolute obedience, exemplified in our Lord who loved not his life, even unto death. And we should open ourselves to the absolute consolation we receive from God, imaged in Mary, Our Lady, the human sign of God's loving kindness that is poured out upon us like the air we breathe, captured magically in Hopkins' great poem, 'The Blessed Virgin Compared to the Air We Breathe':

> *Be thou then, O thou dear*
> *Mother, my atmosphere;*
> *My happier world, wherein*
> *To wend and meet no sin;*
> *Above me, round me lie*
> *Fronting my froward eye*
> *With sweet and scarless sky;*
> *Stir in my ears, speak there*
> *Of God's love, O live air,*
> *Of patience, penance, prayer:*
> *World-mothering air, air wild,*
> *Wound with thee, in thee isled,*
> *Fold home, fast fold thy child.*[1]

[Originally used at the Haddington Pilgrimage 1988.]

1   Gerald Manley Hopkins: *Poems* (Oxford University Press: Oxford).

University Mission

But God proves his love for us in that while we still were sinners Christ died for us.

~ Romans 5:8 ~

I PREACHED here in March and mentioned the fact that when I was 14 I decided I wanted to be a priest, so they sent me to a theological borstal run by mad monks in the Midlands. The monks who ran it were an entertaining and eccentric lot. I was particularly fond of Father Edmund. He was a small teddy bear of a man, with a large unruly stomach that looked like a baking bowl beneath his cassock. He never quite knew which end of the stomach to put his girdle round. If he wound it over the top it made him look like a pregnant cherub; but if he wrapped it under the stomach it invariably slipped down to his ankles and tripped him up. He was loved not only for his eccentricities, but for his loving kindness. One never felt judged by Edmund or found wanting. But his good nature laid him open to persecution. And there was one major weakness that brought out the psychological bully in students who are probably all Archdeacons by now. Edmund had a weak bladder. He lectured in Old Testament, but I do not recall him ever finishing a lecture. He was asthmatic and spoke in short bursts in a sort of snoring delivery: 'The quail ... a foolish bird ... flies too close to the ground ... is therefore easily caught.' But he was never allowed to finish a lecture.

Students would sit at the back of the lecture room with two tumblers under the desk and they would quietly, almost subliminally, pour water from one glass to the other. Slowly, subtly, inexorably, it had its effect. Edmund would start to shift uncomfortably, a look of mild distress would come over his features and he would bring the lecture to a speedy end and trot abstractedly from the room.

Then there was Father Stephen, Edmund's complete opposite. He was tall and austere, with a face like an eagle. His look was piercing. We called him 'Yahweh', and he had the same effect on us that Yahweh had on the children of Israel. He made us feel inadequate, spiritually feeble, morally and intellectually undeveloped. He always induced in me a mood of compulsive self-examination and a fear that he could see into my soul and penetrate to my grubby little secrets. He, too, was asthmatic, but he spoke in controlled bursts of speech, lion-like in their fierce intensity. And he had a strange habit of pawing the ground with his right foot, like a war horse, eager for battle.

The interesting thing was that I thought Stephen was the better Christian, the real man of God, the model of spiritual authenticity. God made me feel sinful, wanting, a failure who could never do enough, never satisfy the divine passion for holiness. And that was the effect Stephen had on me. Why could I not be like him? Why was I not terrific and holy and frightening? Why was I not an eagle of God, hovering over the tiny, transfixed creatures below, scurrying to escape from the scoop of my talons? Stephen filled me with guilt and awe. Edmund filled me with joy, gave me the sense that I was loved, that it was all right, that I was accepted.

Now, of course, I realise that I'd got things the wrong way round. Edmund was the real exemplar of Christianity, not Stephen. And it is important to understand why. There is much in the Bible about right conduct, morality, holiness. It is not surprising, therefore, that people have assumed that Christianity is about a particularly rigorous type of morality. The word 'Christian' has become an adjective that describes a type of behaviour, a way of acting that is self-denying, self-effacing, heroic in its purity and uncomplicated certainty about what is right and what is wrong.

Recently a little episode in my own life confirms this prevailing view of Christianity. My son lives out in the country near Gifford in

East Lothian and I visited him some time ago on a Sunday afternoon, on my way back from a church service, wearing my clerical collar. Recently a family has moved into one of the cottages on the same farm and the children in the family have grown fond of Mark. When they saw me they were intrigued by the funny collar I was wearing. Like a lot of children in our society, they have not the faintest clue about Christianity or the Church. I might have been from another planet. The little boy asked his mother what I was. 'He's a Church man,' she said. 'What's that, what's a church?' Struggling to answer, she said, 'It means you have to watch your Ps and Qs.' My heart sank, of course, but it confirms what I've been saying. People think Christianity is a sort of moral police force, sent into the world to make people mind their Ps and Qs, behave themselves. One of the most dispiriting experiences for ordained ministers is the depressing effect they have on human conviviality. Walk into a party with a collar on, walk into a pub, walk into a rowdy railway compartment, and the effect is like sending a policeman into an illegal nightclub – panic and an immediate attempt to change the subject, shove the illegal substance under the carpet and get out the China tea. It's the Stephen effect. And it's quite tragically wrong.

Christianity is obviously interested in how people behave, because it is interested in human happiness and helping people to grow, but that is not its primary message. Its main and only really important message is that 'While we were yet sinners Christ died for us'. That means that God's love is first and guaranteed. It is poured out upon us freely, extravagantly. We do not have to earn it. We do not have to buy or qualify for God's love by the way we behave. It comes first and last and for ever. It is a gift. That's why we call the Christian message 'good news', not good advice. It is mainly about what God has done for us and only then about how we might respond to God. The motive for Christian conduct is gratitude, not fear. Loved like that, how can we not try to love in return? We need Stephen, of course, but Edmund has to come first. As John puts it, 'We love, we are able to love, only because we are first loved, utterly accepted in our weakness and sinfulness'. Once we really believe that, once it has sunk into our hearts, we discover the security that is the basis on which holiness and goodness can root and grow. If we do not have that sense of security in the certainty of God's accepting love, we won't be capable of spiritual and moral growth. We love when we know we are loved. Edmund comes first. It is the loving-kindness of God that is the first and main message of Christians.

Last Sunday morning I preached at the opening of the first pub church in Scotland. The manager had recently become a Christian and when it was suggested that an act of worship might be offered there before Happy Hour each Sunday, he jumped at the chance. In order to get the word out we issued a press release, hoping the local papers might give it a mention. We were staggered by the response. Phone calls came in from every paper in the country, radio stations and Sky TV. The American Broadcasting Company phoned from New York. They all said the same thing: 'How come you're taking the Church to a pub? Aren't they mutually contradictory? People in churches don't go to pubs and vice versa. OK, I get it. You're going along to preach temperance, tell them to get out of there and come to Church!'

We patiently explained that Church was not a place but a people, and it had a message that was good news, not good advice. It met people where they are and shared with them the love of God. We were going to the pub because the pub wouldn't come to us.

When Sunday morning came the place was packed out with worshippers and with media people. It was a genuine act of worship, moving, challenging and happy. The media people were intrigued, but they still couldn't get it out of their heads that Christians didn't do this kind of thing. We were a moral police force, sent into the world to make people feel guilty, mind their Ps and Qs.

It's enough to make you weep, but we only have ourselves to blame. We have taken the great gospel of God's love and turned it into a stone of offence. Christianity is filled with challenge and it calls us to turn our hearts to God and surrender our lives to God's guiding and submit to God's transforming power, but the energy behind that process is the energy of grateful love and not guilty fear; it is the

Father of the Prodigal Son getting out the best robe and putting it on his wandering boy; it is the Rich Man giving a feast and sending his servants out to the poor parts of the city to invite the hungry to an endless banquet; it is the love of God meeting us in our need and saying, 'You are mine and I love you as you are, but I long for you to grow, to find the happiness of true holiness, so receive my Spirit of power into your life, so that you will soar like an eagle in your charity and goodness, in your love for me and my children, in your care for my creation'.

If we believed that and lived that, we'd undermine this false idea of Christianity that is around, this depressing rumour that we are out to make people miserable. So I pray that just a wee touch of the extravagance of God will grab us during this Mission and I pray double that you will feel in your hearts this day that you are loved with an everlasting love which will hold you close to God's great heart, now and to ages of ages. Amen.

[Originally used at the Glasgow University Chapel, January 1994.]

OCCASIONS

Marriage

Wives, be subject to your husbands, as to the Lord.

~ Ephesians 5:22 ~

I DISCOVERED years ago that organists working in the crematorium business run a sort of musical chart system, a funeral industry Top of the Pops. In Scotland 'Abide with me' is always No. 1 in funeral requests, 'The Lord's My Shepherd' (tune to Crimond) No. 2, and after that the list fluctuates. A great favourite is 'By Cool Siloam's Shady Rill', and it is said that a man from Glasgow planning his mother's funeral asked the organist to play 'By cool salaami'!!

And over the years I've been preparing people for marriage I've noticed that there's a sort of Top of the Pops in Bible readings requested, as well as in hymns. I Corinthians 13 is clearly the No. 1 request and in America the passage from The Song of Solomon – 'Many waters cannot quench love' – was also very popular. Equally of interest were the passages that were increasingly 'dis-requested', if I can coin a word, and the text I have quoted from Ephesians clearly headed that list. Very few girls nowadays want to hear St Paul pleading with them to be subject to their husbands, and most of them ask nervously if they have to say they'll obey their husbands when they are exchanging vows. Most people entering marriage today see it as a partnership of equals in which there may be a proper division of labour and decision-making, but on the basis of equality, not subjection. So poor old Paul is Top of the Pops for his hymn to love, but bottom of the poll for promoting the subordination of women to their husbands. But to attack Paul because he did not

espouse twentieth century attitudes to marriage is historically illit-
erate. Each generation in history is selective in its pursuit of virtue
and in its commitment to truth, and just as each generation imagines
itself to be more intelligent than the one that went before it, and
wiser than the one that comes after it, so it imagines itself to be
more virtuous than both its predecessors and successors. In fact
we all pick and choose. There are fashionable virtues as well as
fashionable vices, though we usually only notice the vices of our
forbears. And Paul is a case in point. It is silly to be angry at him
because he had not read Germaine Greer. What we ought to be doing
is feeling gratitude and astonishment that he helped to develop a
new attitude to marriage in the ancient world that treated the
woman as a person and not just as a chattel; and treated marriage,
not just as a convenient contract, but as a holy estate, a relationship
so important that it could only be compared with Christ's relationship
to the Church. Marriage is a notoriously difficult relationship to
sustain, but Paul was right in seeing it in vocational terms, as a
particular way of living the Christian life. I want to suggest three
ways in which the married state can be seen as a way of holiness, a
pattern of spirituality.

1 *Marriage is a school of Christian love.* Most marriages begin as
   a result of what is called 'erotic' love. Don't be put off by the
   word '*erotic*', it means much more than sexual love. Erotic love
   means a love that needs, a love that wants to receive. I need the
   other person, need to draw her into myself. There is a possessive quality about erotic love. It is like a sponge: it absorbs the
   other, soaks the other into oneself, fills all the empty lonely
   places in one's being. It is the kind of love behind all the love
   songs that ever were. History is filled with the needs and longings
   of erotic love. Men and women are never complete in themselves. They need other men and women to fill up their lack.
   That is erotic love. It is a great and good form of love. And
   most marriages begin on this level. You know that the other
   person completes you; you feel his or her absence as almost a

physical pain. You know that you cannot live without them.

This is the kind of love that gets us married; but it cannot keep us married. It gets us into the air; but it cannot keep us there. Only 'Christian' love can do that. A contrast with erotic love will help us to understand Christian love. There were two important things we saw about erotic love: it was based on need and attraction, and it was like a sponge, it soaked into itself what it needed from the other person. Christian love is the reverse. It is not, for instance, based on attraction. We are not just to love people when we need them or are attracted to them – that's easy. No, we are to love them when we dislike them, disagree with them, are repelled by them. Indeed, we are to love them when they are our enemies. Christian love is not like a sponge, absorbing the other into itself; it is like a mountain stream, endlessly pouring itself out in active benevolence. It's an active, outgoing love – like God's love for us and one of the best places to learn and practise this kind of love is in the married state. Here we are constantly faced with another human being who needs our love and our understanding, not when we feel like it or when they are being particularly lovable, but constantly – for better for worse, for richer for poorer, in sickness and in health. There is no better school for learning the supreme Christian virtue of love than in the school of marriage. '*Love is patient; love is kind and envies no one. Love is never boastful, nor conceited, nor rude; never selfish, nor quick to take offence. Love keeps no score of wrongs; does not gloat over another man's sins, but delights in the truth.*' That is Christian love, and marriage is a place where we can learn much about this supernatural virtue.

2   *Marriage is also a school of self-denial.* The married have to deny themselves many of the pleasures of the world. Most of their money goes, not on themselves, but on their children. Holidays are planned, not for themselves, but for their children. For years they resign their homes and even the kind of clothes they wear to the rule of grubby hands and muddy shoes. All of

this calls for self-denial and almost supernatural patience. And there is more. Marriage is a choice, but like every choice it is also a rejection. Marriage is a choice but it is also a forsaking. Each person is asked in the wedding service to forsake all others and keep only unto their partner. Marriage is a genuine form of self-denial. This is negatively attested to by the difficulty extremely selfish people experience in either getting or staying married. You forsake the patterns of the past and many of the possibilities of the future when you enter the married state. You deny many of the little freedoms you once treasured, for the sake of a larger joy. And in this marriage is a parable of the whole Christian life, for in that life we deny ourselves many things for the sake of the joy that is set before us. So marriage is a school of self-denial.

3   Finally, *marriage is a school of faith*. One of the things all people crave in this life is security and belonging. Marriage is one of the most successful forms of security offered by life. There is nothing quite like the warmth of belonging to a family, the security of love. And yet time passes. I often used to find myself watching my children at sleep or at play. There is an exquisite vulnerability about children. You wrap them in your own strength and you want time to stand still and contain you in that moment, in the deep security of love.

But the day comes when your children have to go out on their own search. Their search may take them to the ends of the earth; it may take them deep into unhappiness or despair. And you can only stand by, powerless in love. The greatest pain of all is when they go before us into death. The death of a child, at any age, is an almost unbearable grief to a parent. No parent can escape the endless wistfulness that goes hand in hand with the joy that children can bring. There is no lasting security here. And even your partner doesn't provide you with everlasting security. Here, again, it is death that steals our joy from us. This fact comes upon us in marriage with devastating certainty. All marriages end in death and separation. My father-in-law in his sermon on marriage used to quote a very sentimental poem about this, but like many sentimental things it strikes a genuine chord of sorrow and hope:

A little way to walk with you, my own,
    Only a little way;
Then one of us must weep and walk alone
    Until God's day.

A little way! It is so sweet to live together
    That I know
Life would not have one withered rose to give
    If one of us should go.

And if these lips should ever learn to smile
    With thy heart far from mine,
'Twould be for joy that in a little while
    They would be kissed by thine.[1]

Marriage reminds us of our own mortality. '*Remember man that dust thou art and unto dust shalt thou return.*' We try to forget that. We try to achieve an easy confidence in ourselves. Marriage teaches us that all flesh is grass. It teaches us that we can have no confidence in ourselves alone. And it thrusts us upon God, who alone is able to save us from destruction. Marriage teaches us to trust in the resurrection of the dead with trembling certainty. It is a school of faith, reminding us of our precariousness, teaching us about our need for God.

A school of love. A school of self-denial. A school of faith. Paul was right to see Christian marriage as a parable of salvation, as a little church, given for the sanctification of life. The Mothers' Union has witnessed to the centrality and sanctity of marriage and the family for years. Marriage has changed in many ways in recent decades, as we have seen, and it has changed for the better, I think

– more open, less oppressive, more balanced and forgiving; and the Mothers' Union has changed with it, but beneath the changes the central thing abides, the reality that points to marriage as a parable of the joys and struggles of Christian life.

- A school of love;
- A school of self-denial;
- And a school of faith in the Resurrection and the life of the world to come.

[Originally used at the Mothers' Union Provincial Centenary Thanksgiving Service, St Mary's Cathedral, Edinburgh, January 1988.]

1   Source unknown.

Ordination of a Deacon

ONE of John Betjeman's most characteristic and endearing poems is called 'Blame the Vicar':

When things go wrong it's rather tame
To find we are ourselves to blame,
It gets the trouble over quicker
To go and blame things on the Vicar.
The Vicar, after all, is paid
to keep us bright and undismayed.

As is usual with Betjeman, underneath the comic verse there is a strongly serious purpose and it illustrates one of the dilemmas that face the ordained minister:

For what's a Vicar really for
Except to cheer us up, What's more,
He shouldn't ever, ever tell
If there is such a place as Hell,
For if there is it's certain he
Will go to it as well as we.[1]

This dilemma is felt with particular force in the task of preaching to which the ordained person is called. How is the preacher to find a proper balance in preaching between the genuine cheerfulness of the Gospel – ' … what's a Vicar really for except to cheer us up' – and the awful demands of Christ? Hitting the balance is not easy and it can only be judged over a long period.

I know whereof I speak because I have been challenged on the subject on several occasions. For instance, some months after I started preaching at the Church of the Advent in Boston in 1980, a delegation from the congregation came to see me to express their concern about my sermons. Now, preachers owe it to their people as well as to their own honour to be careful about how they preach. There is a proper professionalism demanded of the preacher, no less than of the doctor or lawyer. The grace of ordination does not give the preacher the right to inflict sloppy and unprepared utterances upon long-suffering congregations.

That however was not why I was approached on these occasions. It was not the form of my sermons that was being reproached, but the tone and content. In a word, it was felt that I was unduly emphasising the severe side of Christianity, at the expense of the great comfort of the Gospel. My sermons, apparently, were having a depressing effect upon some people, who had nicknamed me 'Father Calvin'. I said several things in reply to this criticism. I replied, first of all, that you could not judge anyone's preaching for breadth and emphasis, unless you listened to him or her preach for a whole year of the Christian calendar. The reason for this was that the Christian Gospel was so wide and paradoxical a teaching, that it could never be expressed in its fulness at any one time. It was a thing of blinding light and frightening darkness, of stern judgement and absolute consolation. Christians were not only assured of the forgiveness of sins for those who truly repented, they were also exhorted to follow Christ in the way of holiness. The Gospel, in short, held as much terror as consolation. To emphasise one at the expense of the other was to mutilate the Gospel. All had to be held together in a sort of passionate equilibrium. Finally, I said that something of the preacher's own nature and its struggles inevitably came through the preaching. According to the scriptures, preaching is a perilous occupation. The bible saves its harshest condemnation for what it calls 'false prophets' – those who give people what they want to hear – false comfort, when they should be alerting them to the lateness of the hour and the dangers facing them. It is a dishonesty to which ordained ministers are particularly prone. They want to be loved. They want to be popular, so they are tempted to avoid, or smooth over the rough places of the Gospel. And not only to make it easier for others. They do it for themselves. They read the scriptures and find themselves wanting; small wonder, therefore, that they are easily tempted to ignore the wintry summons of God and preach only about the gentle springtime of his love. They celebrate the *gift* of God, but rarely acknowledge the chilling demand of Christ to seek after the very perfection of God. Maybe, I said to my gentle critics, I was so afraid of being a false prophet, of lulling people into a false sense of security, that I occasionally overdid the heavy stuff. It was probably, I concluded, my own sense of guilt about my own failures in discipleship that made me overcompensate, by emphasising the awful demands of the Gospel. I was, in short, mostly preaching at myself.

Now, I think about that episode as I meditate upon Paul's letter to the Philippians, and especially upon the passage read as this morning's epistle. Philippians is the most joyful and tender of Paul's letters; nevertheless, it is shot through with the clear call to self-denial and holiness of life. In much of his writing, Paul opposes two distortions of the Christian position, and they are just as prevalent now as they were then. Each is a kind of complacence, which has excised the ingredient of struggle from the Christian life. The first version of this is a kind of triumphant Puritanism. This kind of Christian feels he or she has already arrived at Christian maturity. This is often because of some kind of overwhelming emotional experience. Such people feel born-again, in some sense already made perfect, already saved. There may, indeed, have been a dramatic change in their lives, so they are tempted to feel that the spirit of Christ has already sanctified them and triumphed over their human nature. There were people like that in Paul's day, and there are many of them around today. They exude an aura of triumphant self-satisfaction. *They* are aboard the ship of salvation, while the rest of us poor beggars are hopelessly adrift. Against all this, Paul places his own experience. He tells us that *he* has not yet arrived at full Christian maturity. 'Not that *I* have already obtained this or am already perfect; but I press on to make it my own, because Christ Jesus has made me his own. Brethren, I do not consider that I have made it my own; but one thing I do, forgetting what lies behind and straining forward to what lies ahead, I press on toward the goal for the prize of the upward call of God in Christ Jesus' (Philippians

3:12-14). For Paul, salvation was not something he already had in his pocket. It was a race which he was eagerly running. The super-saved Christians feel they don't need to run. They've already got the gold-medal, so they swan around in their celestial tracksuits, pouring on that winning smile. 'Not so,' thunders Paul. 'The prize is before us, not round our necks. Let us so run as to win it.'

At the other end of the stadium (in riotous disarray) lie the other crowd Paul inveighs against. These don't claim that they have already won salvation, and are now made perfect. Their type of complacence is the opposite of that. They claim that they don't need to make the effort, because Christ has already made it for them. They are the 'un-holier than thou' group, the antinomians, the lawless, the libertines, who believe that Christ has absolved them from all effort and struggle. They can do just what they please, since Christ has already won forgiveness for them. 'Not so,' thunders Paul again. 'Brethren,' he says, 'join in imitating me, and mark those who so live as you have an example in us. For many, of whom I have often told you and now tell you even with tears, live as enemies of the cross of Christ. Their end is destruction, their god is the belly, and they glory in their shame, with minds set on earthly things' (Philippians 3:17-19). Awful words: 'enemies of the Cross of Christ', men and women who do not let the spirit of Christ crucified challenge their weak-nesses.

Paul warns against two types of distortion: the distortion of those who feel they have already made the effort and won the prize; and the distortion of those who feel they are not called upon to make any effort, since it has all been done for them. Puritans and Anti-puritans. They are both a bore. The ones who've never been drunk, and the ones who are hardly ever sober. 'Cut it out,' says Paul, 'there's a race on, and you are meant to be in it. You are neither to stand around, striking attitudes of spiritual superiority, nor are you to lie around in dissolute idleness, you are to run the race with joyful eagerness. Brethren, join in imitating me .... I press on toward the goal for the prize of the upward call of God in Christ Jesus.'

As is often the case in the life of the Christian, the secret is the gift of balance, so that the full, paradoxical range of Christianity can be expressed. Christianity is a merciful religion, but it is also a severe religion. It offers us absolute acceptance and consolation, but it also calls us to holiness, to seek after the very perfection of God. It is easier to go for one of these apparent opposites, rather than hold them both together in a creative tension, to become a soggy liberal or a harsh conservative, a preacher of mercy or a preacher of judgement. Jesus combined both: absolute mercy and absolute demand. And Paul, as we have seen, exactly captures the same tension. This tension is felt by all Christians, but it is felt with particular fierceness by the ordained Christian, the Christian called, like Jennifer, to exercise leadership in the Christian community.

Jennifer, you will find balance a difficult thing to achieve, both in your public service of the Christian family and in your own life of private devotion. You will be tempted to be both too tough on yourself and too easy on yourself, and too tough on your people and too easy on them. Find the balance, discover the secret of what C S Lewis called 'severe mercy', the ability to challenge and inspire others without discouraging them or making them feel that the high aspiration of Christian perfection was beyond them. And you will find that balance in your public ministry only if *you* find it in your private relationship with Jesus. You will constantly remember your frailties, your sins, your unworthiness and weaknesses, and so, touched with infirmity yourself, you will be tender towards the weakness of others. But you have also been caught by a vision of the great holiness of Jesus as the pattern of fulfilled humanity and you will seek to follow Christ in the way of perfection; and so, inspired by the perfection of Christ you will want to call your people to the perfection of their own natures, you will be ambitious for them to grow in Christian maturity and understanding. It's all in the balance. May Christ who called you, give you that wisdom, so that you may, in your ministry, show forth both the mercy and majesty of Christ.

[Originally used at St Peter's, Musselburgh, January 1989. This was at the ordination to the Diaconate of Jennifer Jones.]

1   John Betjeman: *Collected Poems* (John Murray Publishers Ltd: London).

Ordination to the Priesthood

Jacob was left alone; and a man wrestled with him until daybreak. When the man saw that he did not prevail against Jacob, he struck him on the hip socket; and Jacob's hip was put out of joint as he wrestled with him. Then he said, 'Let me go, for the day is breaking.' But Jacob said, 'I will not let you go, unless you bless me'.

So he said to him, 'What is your name?' And he said, 'Jacob'. Then the man said, 'You shall no longer be called Jacob, but Israel, for you have striven with God and with humans, and have prevailed.' Then Jacob asked him, 'Please tell me your name'. But he said, 'Why is it that you ask my name?' And there he blessed him. So Jacob called the place Peniel, saying, 'For I have seen God face to face, and yet my life is preserved'.

~ Genesis 32:24-31 ~

THE bits of the Bible I like best are the Zen bits, the teasing, opaque passages that don't shout their meaning at us, but leave us puzzled and disturbed, yet strangely excited. They operate like the sentences Zen masters give their disciples. They disarm us, de-skill us and tantalise us with hints of a compelling mystery not quite revealed. This is the way I feel about the passage in Genesis chapter 32 where Jacob wrestles with the divine stranger. Jacob himself is a strange topic for an ordination service. The only selection conference he would get through would be the process for selecting Tory Parliamentary candidates. Jacob, after all, was a sort of proto-Thatcherite, who schemed his way to great wealth and made lots of enemies in the process. Yet here he is at the heart of this mysterious

104

and compelling passage. But it's as well for some people to remember that God has a right wing as well as a left. Anyway, I gain enormous comfort from the sacred villains of holy scripture.

The next thing that strikes me about this passage is that it shows us that God challenges us to wrestle with the divine mystery, and the struggle is a bit like lovemaking. It is an attempt to enter and know, in some sense to subdue the divine stranger who so easily slips out of our clutches. It's not always easy to justify the existence of the clergy, but there's no way of justifying them if they do not struggle with God in prayer and thought, in a sort of erotic bafflement. We should be God's lovers and there should be something of the danger and obsessiveness of a love affair in our life with God. The last thing it should be is dull and boring like a dead marriage. It should be a fling, a grand affair, something that dominates and obsesses us. I am reminded of what Harold Talbot wrote about Thomas Merton's Asian journey:

> *He tipped Sikh taxi drivers like a Proustian millionaire. He was on a roll, on a toot, on a holiday from school. He was a grand seigneur, a great lord of the spiritual life. He woke people up and enchanted them and gave them tremendous happiness and a good laugh. People knew his spiritual quality. People in planes knew it. There was no question about it. Merton was not an object of scrutiny, he was an event.*

We should so give ourselves to God that we are captured by God's recklessness and generosity, the way Merton was, the way great souls always are.

The next thing to notice is that this struggle with God wounds us – and I'm not talking about the wounded healer phenomenon, the recognition that we are flawed and that we minister as much from weakness as strength. That has all become a bit of a cliché and I take it absolutely for granted. No, I'm talking about the wounds we receive as a consequence of our helpless fascination with God, this inability to get out of God's clutches. Women have been more gravely wounded than men in this struggle.

The debate about the ordination of women in our Church has been a strange affair. On the one hand it has been a debate about theology, about the nature of authority, about women in the abstract. But there are *no* women in the abstract. There is only Elizabeth, and Jane, and Rosemary, and Alison, and Pamela – actual women with feelings and needs, longings and hopes; and they, many of them, have been deeply wounded by the years of struggle, because it has been for them not an interesting theological debate, not an exercise in ecclesiological reformation, but a felt injustice, a quite personal pain, an institutionalised rejection, an actual oppression. That is why many good women have lost patience and left us. It is why Daphne Hampson now believes that Christianity and its God are intrinsically and incurably sexist, by definition misogynistic. This is a day of rejoicing and celebration, but we must not take it cheaply and easily in our stride. We must confess that for too long women have been wounded in the house of their friends and the whole Church has been limping in pain till this day. So this day, as a male bishop and a company of male priests lay their hands on the patient heads of their sisters to incorporate them into the company of Presbyters, must also be seen as a day of healing and penitence for the long years of wounding.

Sadly, new wounds appear as we heal the old ones. There are those for whom our work today will bring pain. It is a pain I cannot understand, but it is a pain I must acknowledge and find, if possible, ways to assuage. Struggling with the mystery of God hurts. There seems to be no escape from the pain but one of the foundational paradoxes of our faith is that we are healed by Christ's great wounding.

And then after he was wounded by God Jacob was named Israel, the one who strives.

God calls us *in* the struggle and the wounding. God does not call us out of it. Most of us subscribe to a displacement theory of the divine will. We feel we are meant to be somewhere else, in some state of prayer or understanding or maturity or peace where we'll finally find God. It's always somewhere else where we'll be someone else. But God's not interested in these fantasies. He calls us and blesses us where we are now, just as he is calling these friends of ours in all their muddled and wounded humanity to receive the blessing of priesthood. This is what it all comes down to. We are blessed that we might bring that blessing to others, *be* that blessing. But what is it, that blessing? It is only the Gospel. And what is the Gospel? It is only forgiveness. That's what this is all about. The world's need of forgiveness, your need, my need. It's the only really useful thing a priest can do, to tell people they are already forgiven.

The American novelist Frederick Buechner captures this movingly in his novel, *The Final Beast*. In the story, Rooney, troubled by an act of adultery in her past, has run away. Her priest goes after her and finds her in the home of her friend Lillian, who speaks to him while Rooney is upstairs:

'Oh Lord, how advice bores me, especially when it's good. And yours was good enough. "Go back to your husband." That probably didn't come so easy, did it? "Forgive your infidelity" .... It's so modern, and it's so sane, and it's just the advice she'd want if she wanted advice. Only give her what she really wants .... '

'Give her what, for Christ's sake?'

'For Christ's sake .... The only thing you have to give.' And then she almost shouted at him. 'Forgive her for Christ's sake, little priest!'

'But she knows I forgive her.'

'She doesn't know God forgives her. That's the only power you have – to tell her that. Not just that he forgives the poor little adultery. But the faces she can't bear to look at now. The man's. Her husband's. Her own, half the time. Tell her God forgives her for being lonely and bored, for not being full of joy with a house full of children. That's what sin really is, you know – not being full of joy. Tell her that sin is forgiven whether she knows it or not, that's

*what she wants more than anything else – what all of us want. What
on earth do you think you were ordained for?'*

SHEILA
JANET
DIANA
ALISON
CLEPHANE
ELIZABETH
JENNIFER
MARY PAT
ELIZABETH
FRANCES
JANE
JOLYON
CAROL
ROSEMARY
HENDY
ISABEL
PAMELA

**Go out and tell this sad, old world that it is forgiven.
That's what it is waiting to hear
and that's why you are being sent.**

[Originally used at St Mary's Cathedral, Edinburgh, on 17 December
1994, the day the first women were ordained to the priesthood in the Scottish
Episcopal Church.]

Consecration of a Bishop

WHEN I lived in Boston in the USA I used to take a walk on Sunday afternoons to a park by the Charles River close to the rectory. I was drawn to one place in particular, because roller skaters from all over Boston congregated there, with their own personal stereos clamped to their heads, and they would dance and gyrate to music no one else could hear. I became obsessed by one large lady in fishnet tights, all ruffled and bowed, about my own age, who more or less stood there and quivered to some inner music. They all appeared to be oblivious to the large crowd that gathered to watch them, yet they were clearly there to be seen. I was struck by the ambiguity of it all. In fact, much about American life was having a perplexing effect on me. Looking back, I can see I was in a state of culture shock: the language was the same but the meanings were different. For instance, ordinands perplexed me. In Scotland I had always been pleased to help ordinands discover a vocation to the ministry, from the first shy reference to the possibility, right up to the moment of ordination. But in the US it was different. There was no shyness. They walked into my office and sold themselves, showed me why the Church couldn't afford to overlook their skills and gifts and would I please chase the bishop along because he seemed not to realise that this particular candidate was God's answer to all our problems. 'What extraordinary conceit,' I would think to myself, 'how can I possibly commend people for ordination with such inflated opinions of themselves?'

In my perplexity I started reading about the cultural differences between America and Britain. I remember reading a book called

Showing Off in America, which set out to demonstrate that America, unlike Britain, went in for overstatement and that Americans were taught to go out and sell themselves, to think positively, to go for it, to walk confidently onto the stage. In Britain the cultural style is the obverse of that, so it's easy for Brits to think that Yanks are cosmically conceited, if not outright liars. What I had to do was learn to read the cultural language and get inside their system rather than translate it, unflatteringly, into mine. I should have twigged earlier, anyway, because human beings are always signalling to one another, and even people that use the same code misread each other. We are enmeshed in a network of symbols and signs, and we can be too pre-occupied or insensitive to interpret what others are trying to communicate to us. The poet Stevie Smith captured our predicament perfectly when she described someone as 'not waving but drowning'.

If we find it difficult to interpret one another and the signals that pass between us, it is infinitely more difficult to interpret the signals that come from God. The network of sign and symbol that communicates God's mystery to us is called, in theological shorthand, Revelation, God's showing off to us, God's way of getting our attention. This is the main theme of this day. The very word Epiphany means a showing off, an attempt to get attention, and like every other mode of communication it has to be interpreted and is open to misunderstanding. Revelation is always ambiguous, because God uses signs we think we already understand, but we have difficulty penetrating to the inner meaning. 'Is not this the carpenter's son? What can we possibly learn from him?' And we miss the moment, fail to encounter the divine. It is our familiarity with the things God uses to signal to us that is our biggest danger. A revelation always comes through something we know, but it is something else as well, something we don't know, and what we think we know gets in the way of what we do not yet know. There is no way round this puzzle. It characterises our relationships with one another and with God. Always there is this ambiguously familiar event that can, if we'll let it, disclose something new to us, give us a sudden hint of God's glory.

This principle of loaded ambiguity applies to the ordained ministry. Through ordination God uses a particular humanity as a mode of divine expression. And the humanity both expresses and obscures the revelation; it is the carrier of the divine but it is always also something else as well. The main tension in ministry comes from living with the knowledge that it is our humanity that God uses, and that we must not call common what God has made holy. In ministry there is an inescapable tension between self-acceptance and self-surrender. The office of bishop probably heightens this ambiguity more than in any other order of ministry. It is a universal office, an office in the whole Church, but its mode of expression is always quite specific to the individual.

Douglas will be a quite specific type of bishop. This is one reason why he should have no anxiety about the job. He, as he is, is called to be a bishop, to allow his given humanity to be the mode of God's communication with his children. It is his actual humanity that will be so used, not some off-the-shelf version that he must try to fit himself into. By being himself, Douglas will be your bishop. As a matter of fact, Douglas already has a formidable list of episcopal characteristics. He is a man of depth and utter dependability, but his strength is not the unimaginative strength of the merely self-confident. He can strengthen others, because he has been strengthened himself. He can understand others, because he has himself been understood. His own strong humanity has experienced the grace and love of God, and it is that surrendered humanity that God will use in his ministry.

The main element in the ministry of bishops is their own humanity, but the office itself and the things that have to be done have their own built-in ambiguity. Bishops are called to be leaders in a community whose founder expressed a radical mistrust of power. How do we exercise leadership in a way that conforms to Christ and not to the world? Christian leadership is far from being an exact science and it is something that is always intrinsically flawed, but I think the secret lies in the motivation. God uses our humanity and its limitations, but we must surrender it to God in a way that will allow God to transcend it. For instance, if a bishop is a normally strong and decisive person, God may want him to find his gentler side, the side that can co-operate with others. If he is by nature gentle, maybe even indecisive, God may have to help him discover a source of strength that will enable him to make decisions. Whatever the temperament, choices are inescapable, and the strong man may have to learn how to make them gently, while the gentle man may have to learn to make them strongly. This is one reason why Christian leaders have to be penitents, have to know themselves deeply, so that they may not always identify their own method and style with God's. Saying their prayers and confessing their sins, they will make choices and live with them, knowing that they will sometimes make the wrong decision and be applauded for it, and sometimes make the right decision and be condemned. This, too, is taken care of by the mercy of God, and it is why we find the strength to make decisions at all, remembering Bonhoeffer's words about our confidence depending on a God 'who demands responsible action in a bold venture of faith and who promises forgiveness and consolation to the man who becomes a sinner in that venture'.

So bishops offer God their humanity and its limitations for the work of ministry and sometimes hard choices have to be made; but the main and most enjoyable part of a bishop's work is the ministry of encouragement. Bishops operate on a wider field than parish priests, but that very fact is their greatest temptation, because it can cause them to forget that the real life and the most important work of the Church goes on in the parishes. Douglas has been an outstanding parish priest for thirty years, so he is not likely to forget that fact. Douglas, be an encourager and strengthener of your clergy and the people in your parishes. There is only one thing more depressing than a priest who constantly gets across his people, and that is a bishop who constantly gets across his clergy. Sometimes it's inevitable – tough choices again – but most of the time it'll be your encouragement they need, your confidence in the work they are doing, sometimes in difficult circumstances. As a matter of fact, this is an aspect of the bishop's work that Douglas is almost uniquely suited to. He will be a pastor to the pastors, someone who cares for the carers. It might help, Douglas, if, like me, you see yourself as a sort of travelling comedian, sent out like entertainers in wartime to cheer people up – that's why in a few minutes I'll give you a funny hat!

Cheering people up – isn't that a noble vocation? It sounds very close to a definition of gospel, good news. Dean Inge said that Christianity was good news, not good advice, the message of God's love for us, not a chorus of disapproval. Douglas, be a sign of God's love in this ancient diocese and, as Alastair Haggart has probably already said to you, not only be a bishop, enjoy being a bishop!

[Originally used at St John's Cathedral, Oban, January 1993. This was at the consecration of Douglas Cameron as Bishop of Argyll & the Isles.]

OCCASIONS

Festival

Lord, are there few that be saved?

~ Luke 13:23 ~

THE last time I preached at a Festival service in Old St Paul's was three years ago on exactly the same Sunday, with exactly the same readings from the Three Year Lectionary. I remember the occasion, because I did not particularly like the Gospel then and I don't much like it today. And I am beginning to suspect that the Rector doesn't much like it either, which is why he's always careful to line me up to preach when it comes round. Like many preachers of a liberal mind and a generous nature, I am uneasy with those bits of the scripture that don't fit my point of view. When I am honest with myself, I have to admit that there is a lot about the Bible that I don't care for. For instance, I'm not keen on the books in the Old Testament that describe the settlement of the Jews in Palestine. The Bible claims that it was God's plan to root out the Canaanites and settle the Israelites in their place, using a process of genocide and ethnic cleansing that is all too familiar today. Human nature is always able to find justifications for its own crimes and excesses, and history teaches us that the best cover for any shady deal is God.

During the Second World War Evelyn Waugh and Randolph Churchill found themselves in Yugoslavia, sharing the same hut, acting as liaison officers to Tito's partisans. Waugh took an instant dislike to Tito and spread the rumour that he was a Lesbian. He was equally bored with Churchill who talked all the time and hindered his work on *Brideshead Revisited*. He discovered that Churchill had never read the Bible so, to keep him quiet, he persuaded him to read it from cover to cover. They would sit in their hut, Waugh correcting the proofs of Brideshead and Churchill wading cheerlessly through the historical books of the Old Testament. From time to time Churchill would look up from his biblical studies and pronounce: 'I say, Evelyn, God is an awful shit.' If even Randolph Churchill was repelled by the blood thirstiness of Jehovah, then most moderate minded people would have to agree that there is a problem. We have a choice. We either take the Bible literally, persuading ourselves that everything it says is divinely inspired, and landing ourselves in a situation where we have to justify the morals of a God who often behaves like a Serbian warlord; or we take it historically, seeing it as the record of the moral and spiritual evolution of humanity, gradually purging its idea of God, till something of God's true nature comes through, however fitfully and episodically, and thereby landing ourselves in a situation where we have to use our own minds and consciences in the inexact art of discerning the nature of God. We either choose ugly certainty or anxious uncertainty; we either read scripture as though it were a fax direct from God or we read it as a spiritual code that needs breaking and interpreting before yielding its meaning for our own lives.

Today's Gospel is a good example of the kind of work we have to do if scripture is to make sense for our lives. The background to the story is ancient, but it is a surprisingly consistent theme in human history. There are various fundamentalist groups in the world, particularly in the USA and in South Korea, who believe in a theory that used to be called predestination. According to this theory, most people have been created by God for destruction and eternal damnation, but some have been chosen for salvation. These are the elect, chosen by God from eternity to enjoy his special favour, while everyone else is on the way to hell. At the end of all things Christ will return, the elect will be taken from among the nations and caught up into what is called the rapture – a period of intense supernatural bliss – which will last for a quite precise period of time, before they are taken finally into heaven. A particular sect in Korea recently announced that the rapture will commence in mid-October, and a number of Korean businessmen are giving up their businesses to prepare for the end. There are similar groups in the USA. Recently I read the classic Scottish novel by James Hogg, *Confessions of a Justified Sinner*. This extraordinary psychological novel is about a young man who believes that he is one of God's elect and chosen, and becomes a serial killer, logically concluding that if the people who interfered with his own plans were destined for final destruction anyway, there was a lot to be said for helping the process on a bit by assisting their descent into hell with a sharp knife.

The background to this kind of theological frenzy is a period in Jewish history, reflected in today's Gospel, when scholars debated the number who would be saved when God sent his messiah to rescue Israel from its oppressors. One first century Jewish author gave a pessimistic answer: 'The Most High made this world for the sake of many, but the world to come, for the sake of the few; many have been created, but few will be saved.' This is the background to the question that someone put to Jesus, 'Lord, are there few that be saved?' Characteristically, Jesus does not answer the question directly. In fact, he does not address the issue of the unsaved at all. He addresses those who think they are saved already, the elect, the ones who are sure they are members of the club. We cannot know the exact context of the saying, but it seems to be one of a group that challenges Jewish exclusiveness, the notion that God is interested only in the Jews. A related theme is the refusal of religious leaders of his time to recognise that in Jesus God was speaking a new word to them, disclosing a new insight into his nature. Beware, Jesus is saying, of beliefs that exclude others from the care of God. Beware of theologies, ideologies, social structures that are based on privilege and exclusion, whether spiritual, racial or economic. God calls everyone to his Festival. Don't be so sure it's just for you.

In a curious kind of a way there is an annual return of this ancient debate every year in Edinburgh. We ask ourselves: 'Is the Festival for the few or for the many? Is it for the cultured elite or is there something in it for everyone?' This question, like the one put to

Jesus, raises an ancient and important theological issue called 'election'. Given that God had elected the Jews for a special role, was the election a privilege or a responsibility? Was it something they were given for their own sakes or something they were called to for the sake of others? The answer that finally comes through scripture is that all election, all privilege, all special blessings are given for the sake of others. Life's festival is for everyone and we should use our special gifts to widen the joy. I think this happens in the Edinburgh Festival. Sure, there's a lot of highly specialist stuff around and sure the people living in the perimeter housing estates don't exactly trek in to hear Schoenberg at the Usher Hall, but they are not thereby forgotten. In recent Festivals the Grassmarket Project, with its raw theatre of social realism, has made the whole Festival public aware of the homeless, young offenders, the mentally ill, and young women trapped in the sex industry. The voiceless have been given a voice. But no one is saying that the extravagant craziness of the Festival should be closed down and the money poured into social work. No, it is given to us all to enjoy, it is a parable of life itself. But we mustn't fall into the old trap of the elect, of enjoying the privileges we have been given with no thought for those others whom God loves and wishes to serve through us. Jesus never gives philosophical answers to the problems of life: why do the few have much and the many have so little? How can we reconcile the challenge to struggle for human equality with the importance of respecting human freedom? He always turns the question round and says, 'What are you doing about it?' He does it in today's Gospel. That's what makes it uncomfortable, that's why I didn't enjoy thinking about it. That's why when this particular passage comes round again I'll make sure Alan, not I, preaches it. But it's not a bad question to hear in the middle of our rejoicing. 'Lord, are there few that be saved?' He looks at us and replies: 'Supposing the answer is "yes", what are *you* going to do about it?'

[Originally used at Old St Paul's, August 1992, during the Edinburgh International Festival.]

Thanksgiving for Coates Hall

Let us build here three tabernacles.

~ Luke 9:33 ~

IN his biography of Michael Ramsey, Owen Chadwick tells the story of the then Archbishop of Canterbury returning from a visit to one of the Provinces of the Anglican Communion. As the plane descended at Heathrow he looked down gloomily and said, 'I hate the Church of England. I hate the Church of England. I hate the Church of England'. Chadwick suggests that there was a particular reason for his attitude towards the Church which he'd served all his ministry. Though he looked like the Ancient of Days, Ramsey was actually quite a radical figure. He believed that the Church was a living, changing organism, not a preservationist sect. He believed that again and again the Church of England had turned its back on the future God had called it to; so, like Lot's wife, it was in danger of transforming itself into an archeological deposit. He talked about the great Christian centuries to come and, on occasions when he was aroused, he would lift his arms in the air and proclaim, 'We are the early Christians'. He was particularly interested in the evolution of societies and churches, and how changes might best be made in what were, intrinsically, rather conservative institutions. In his book, *The Glory of God and the Transfiguration of Christ*, he used a section of Arnold Toynbee's *Study of History* to help the Church deal with change. Toynbee had argued that a civilisation faced with rapid transition and the possibility of decline can react in four ways: archaism, futurism, detachment or transfiguration.

Archaism is the false idealisation of the past, captured for me in some piercingly nostalgic lines from Kathleen Raine:

If I could turn upon my finger
The bright ring of time
The now of then
I would bring back again.[1]

We need to know something about 'the now of then' and the study and understanding of our own history is an important part of human piety, as well as human curiosity. This is why I welcome Bishop Luscombe's booklet, *A Seminary of Learning: A History of Edinburgh Theological College from 1810-1994*. It's an affectionate portrait of theological training in the Scottish Episcopal Church, and it demonstrates the variety of systems there have been for the formation of clergy for our Church. For instance, the College moved to rented premises at 9 Rosebery Crescent in 1880 and a contemporary description says, 'The buildings were poor, just two students; the teaching staff was limited, and the material equipment not much better than that of a second class board school'. In 1891 however, the Representative Church Council purchased the mansion house of the Napier family, known as Coates Hall, at the west end of Grosvenor Crescent. Bishop Luscombe reminds us that extensive alterations and additions were made to provide rooms for 15 students, as well as a chapel, library, lecture room and dining hall. The total cost was just over £14,000. The College at Coates Hall had its difficulties but, as Bishop Luscombe shows, it was a successful and busy institution for most of this century.

So, it would be tempting for members of the Scottish Episcopal Church to fall into a mood of regret on a day like this: 'Let us build here three tabernacles and stay forever on the Holy Mount,' might be our mood. But human history is an evolutionary experience; it is, in fact, impossible to stay still, even in the same place. After a hundred years at Coates Hall, God is calling us to go out in faith to a place he has prepared for us.

If archaism is a danger for us, then futurism is maybe even a worse danger. The futurist is the direct opposite of the archaist. Futurists have a contempt for the past. They show little gratitude to those who have gone before. They fail to appreciate their debt to those into whose inheritance they have entered. Futurists give off a sense of disconnection and discontinuity. They are unrooted people, careless of our pieties and our affections. They lack the wisdom that understands that change brings loss as well as gain, and must be faced with regret as well as with courage.

Detachment is another way of describing the old spiritual problem of *accedia,* the sickness that destroyeth in the noon day. Middle aged clergy are in particular danger here. There is a kind of cynicism that can overcome clergy in whom the oil has burned dangerously low. Some of them suffer personal crises of faith. Their years of service, apparently unproductive years of labouring in the ministry, can sap their energies.

They say to themselves, 'We have laboured all night and taken nothing', and slide into indifference. They can be identified by their complaining, querulous tone and their general attitude of embittered fatigue.

The fourth and only really creative response is transfiguration. It is close to the evolutionary paradigm that modern science has introduced us to. Human history is a dynamic evolving reality that is always growing from the past in all its loss and wisdom, to new patterns that will, in their turn, change into newer forms. This is the pattern of sacrifice: of dying to the past in order to live; neither repudiating nor clinging to where we have been; recognising the emerging glory and refusing the temptation to camp out permanently on the Holy Mount. For the community of faith, this principle of radical continuity is expressed through our experience of God, who uses, but is not limited by, the instrumentalities of history; as well as through our own history, which is a story of dynamic continuity. This is close to what we mean by anamnesis, which is the permanent duty of the Church to make ever present the reality, not of the dead, but of the living Christ.

Now it is platitudiness to observe that the Scottish Episcopal Church is going through a period of turbulent change. We have come to one of those moments of challenge, and our response will lead us either to decline or to renewed vigour. We could paralyse ourselves into archaism, an entirely backward looking posture that is a kind of disobedience to God's challenge to us in our own day. Remember Lot's wife. Just as dangerous would be a restless and unrooted progressivism that showed no appreciation of the importance of managing change compassionately and constructively. More dangerous still is the third response of detachment. There can be a corrosive cynicism at work in people that is purely destructive. The word 'cynic' comes, of course, from the Greek word for dog, and there is a type of person who, from the safety of the sidelines, yaps away at those who are trying to get on with the job.

I pray that we will have the courage to give ourselves to the painful process of transfiguration, so that God will be able to take our past and mould it into the future he has prepared for us. This is the way of transfiguration; it is the way of Abraham, who obeyed when he was called to leave a place which he had known and loved, for a land of promise he knew nothing of. When I was struggling in 1979 with a call to leave Edinburgh to work in Boston, I consulted a Japanese theologian I knew at the University of Chicago. He looked at me and said, 'No one who has never left his own country to live in another land can really understand the essence of biblical theology, because it is a theology of exile'. To leave a place we have known and loved, and go out into the unknown, is a parable of faith; it is a sign of radical faith in the God who has prepared for us a homeland in his own heart and in no other place.

And the way of transfiguration, of course, is the way of Christ, who has shown us his glory but won't let us settle down on the Holy Mount, in spite of our longing, expressed by Peter, for stability and permanence: 'Let us build here three tabernacles.' We know that on the next day, when they had come down from the mountain, a great crowd met them. Alas, there is no pause button or rewind mechanism in the history of the Church. We cannot stand still or go back. God calls us to new places and new challenges; and the only thing he will promise us is his own presence on the journey.

So, let us thank God that we have been here and seen his glory, and acknowledge that we cannot stay, because we have work to do elsewhere. Arise. Let us depart. God is calling. He has prepared for us another city.

[Originally used at The Theological Institute Thanksgiving Service, May 1994.]

1   Kathleen Raine: *On a Deserted Shore* (Poem 95) (Dolmen Press, Dublin 1973).

The Future of the Church

ON September 21st 1745, William Harper, the minister of St Paul's Chapel in Carrubber's Close in Edinburgh, went to Linlithgow to marry Hugh Smith to Mrs Elizabeth Seton. When he filled up the Register after the service he added this note:

> *Just before this office begun, Mr Charles Smith brought an account of the complete victory obtained this morning at Gladsmuir by the Prince's army over that commanded by General Cope: <u>Doxa to Theo en Hupsistois</u> – Glory to God in the Highest.*

In those days what is now Old St Paul's in Edinburgh's Royal Mile was a centre of Jacobite sympathies, and the sentiments still linger. When Father Lockhart was rector he used to hold a dinner once a year and toast the King over the Water, knowing exactly who the current Pretender to the Throne was. Alas, I must make a public confession and admit that I am not an uncritical admirer of the Stuart line. My head tells me that, with few exceptions, they were a stubborn lot who brought most of their troubles on themselves. Nevertheless, I am in my heart a firm and romantic lover of the Jacobites, though they deserved better men for whom to die. I love Montrose especially, going gallantly to his death. When a puritan railed at him for combing his elegant hair on the scaffold in readiness for his execution, he replied:

> *While my head is my own, I dress and arrange it. Tomorrow when it is yours you may treat it as you please.*

And I love all the romantic literature which the Stuart cause produced. I like to think of the heralds of the risings galloping through the glens, telling men to gird on their claymores because the Prince had landed and his hour had come. So I like to think of Mr Charles Smith leaping on his pony to speed to Linlithgow to tell Mr Harper on September 21st 1745, that the Prince had won a famous victory at Gladsmuir.

We know Mr Smith's name, but nothing else about him. He was a herald, a bearer of tidings, and his message was the important thing. The herald is a significant though anonymous figure in history. It was the herald's job to bring news, tidings of battles won or lost. It was a self-effacing task. The herald did not proclaim any messages of his own; he was strictly instructed in what he had to proclaim, and he went off and did it.

When our Lord and the early Christians wanted to describe the apostolic task of the Church, they used this word 'herald'. It was not the task of Christian missionaries to proclaim themselves or their own ideas. They had a strict commission from their Lord to proclaim the Gospel, the good news of what Christ offered to men and women. If you read the accounts of Paul's missionary journeys in the Acts of the Apostles, or know anything about the history of the expansion of Christianity to every race on earth, it is filled with images of people on the move, heralds on horseback or striding up dusty roads in Asia Minor; it conjures up pictures of men and women in boats, paddling up vast rivers; and for the people of Ireland it will inevitably suggest the coming of Patrick, Herald of the Gospel, Apostle of this island. He arrived in AD 432. By the time of his death in AD 461, the whole island had been converted to what one writer calls 'an elated version of Christianity'. By AD 444 there was already a native ministry and an Episcopal See here in Armagh. There were churches, schools, the beginnings of a monastic life. The sheer joyous energy of his apostolate is staggering and challenging.

But that image of movement and energy is in marked contrast to what most of us think about when we conjure up an image of the Church today. Our image is likely to be a static one, probably a building, a church, a beloved cathedral like this one, filled with memories of peace received, forgiveness known, the presence of God mediated. And that is the paradox of modern Church history: we have these places we love, because once upon a time missionaries like Patrick rode up dangerous roads and crossed perilous rivers to bring the tidings that caused the response that built the buildings. Now these buildings seem to keep the word in, instead of sending it out, so they have become a risk to us. Our buildings have become a parable of our own condition as a Church. They have trapped us in a semi-developed state and they occupy so much of our energies that we are unable to think beyond them and see the new models that are beckoning to us. Let me try to offer you a quick historical summary of how I think we got to where we are before picking up my crystal ball and gazing into the Church's future.

In the Christian movement several things are always going on at the same time, or ought to be. An important aspect of our life is what we might call the gathering of a people, the kind of thing Patrick excelled at. We have a new message for humanity. In Christ, God proclaims a new thing, a new understanding of the Divine nature as unconditional love and eternal mercy. Those first captured by this message, such as Patrick, are compelled, by its sheer power, to share it. They go out into the world as heralds and proclaimers, sharing the good news of what God has done for humanity in Christ. They gather people, they make converts, they create communities. Then two things begin to happen. First of all, they have to care for and organise the people they have gathered and so shape them that they in turn can go out and be themselves heralds who bring the good news to their generation. But something else is always going on at the same time. We are talking about the creation of a Church, the gathering of a people. This Christian reality, this divine institution, always and unavoidably reflects and parallels the surrounding culture. So the Church, which is meant to reflect the kingdom of God and the mind and mercy of God, also begins to reflect the world and its best or most fashionable political models. The community that was meant to reflect the mind of God increasingly mirrors the mind of the world. During its most formative years the Church was surrounded by intensely authoritarian structures and it has, to a very great extent, interiorised this understanding of institutions, this paradigm of government. We have become a mini state with a government and laws, values and customs, and a particular intellectual culture we call theology.

But more and more we realise that this theoretical model of the Church as authoritative truth and institutional permanence is almost comically at variance with the reality we all experience. Indeed, we ought to go much further and say that the model we have borrowed from the state no longer works for the state either. Part of the anguish of British politics at the moment is that all sorts of groups are fighting rear-guard actions against emerging, alternative political models. The old models no longer serve us well, but such is our nostalgia for ancient institutions that we would rather perish with the old than flourish with the new. We are left, therefore, with institutions in Church and State that consume all our energies in maintenance and prevent us from contemplating new possibilities. In the case of the Church, our understandable affection for our buildings is paralleled in the way we organise ourselves into pastoral units. We have long since ceased to be a gathering people, a people on the move through history. We have become a gathered people, settled on a high beach, where we manage and embellish the life we have created for ourselves.

Let me leave that opinion on one side and move to another dynamic element in the Christian tradition. The picture I have given suggests a community going out with a fixed message and gathering people to share it. But that was only ever half the reality. In a crucial verse in John's sixteenth chapter, Christ tells us that God's revelatory activity will never be over. God, he tells us, has new things to teach us that we cannot hear now, but the Holy Spirit will guide us into an understanding of them. In other words, the message of God keeps coming and we are to be alert to the new things God wants to tell us.

Christians have been better at packaging and protecting the old things God has done than at paying attention to and obeying the new word God has for them. The prevailing Christian model in our country sees the Church as the spiritual arm of the National Trust, part of the heritage industry, there to conserve and preserve, to burnish and to cherish, never ever to abandon and move out into pastures new. Yet the main energy of the New Testament is the energy of movement and discovery. It paints a picture of a God who comes, not a God who has already been. Scripture tells us to look for this God, expect to find this God, not in the midst of the licensed assemblies of faith but at the edges, on the margins. It is the Syro Phoenician woman who challenges Jesus and his disciples to share the message of God's love with Gentiles as well as with Jews. It is the Roman non-commissioned officer Cornelius whom God uses to persuade Peter the Managing Director of the Apostles that the Christian Gospel was for all and not just for his cousins in Jerusalem.

What are the implications of this dynamic element in the Christian tradition? It would seem to me that the main implication is that God will be trying to tell the Church something new, and God will be speaking to it from its own edges and from the edges of society. One of the things that seems to be happening in our society is that new political models are being born. The new models are models of community, models that emphasise plurality and mutuality, and the ability of all men and women to play their part in finding structures appropriate to their needs. The old, male-dominated, verticalised, centralised, highly concentrated institution ought to be a thing of the past. It doesn't work, because it alienates people, makes them dependent. Europe itself offers us new and exciting models in which authority is widely diffused into city states, city regions.

It seems to me, therefore, that just as the old Church modelled itself appropriately on the old vertical structures, so I believe the Church of the Future should model itself on these new emerging horizontal structures. We should sit lightly to the institutional model we have inherited and experiment with more human models, models of co-operation which emphasise the plural nature of humanity. If we followed this new model, then the Church's ministry would not be there to rule but to stimulate, to encourage creativity.

We would be the poets and clowns, not the managing directors of the new people of God, and the Church we operated within would be open at the edges. It would be a Church that reflected the untidy reality of faith-seeking and faith-sharing. Church membership would be an invitation to pilgrimage, an invitation to accompany a people on the way, not enrolment in an institution on a fixed site. In the Church of the Future, operating on this new model, there would be radical experiments in Christian living, in liturgy and prayer, in theological exploration, in faith sharing and prophetic witness. We might retain most of our buildings, but they would be resources from which we went out, rather than places into which we insisted on drawing people. Our buildings, too, would be less static in feel and layout. They would reflect this dynamic living reality of God towards whom we are being drawn. They would be places where quietness was a powerful reality as well as creativity; and our clergy would be as famous for their ability to keep silent as for their ability to speak. In other words, the Church of the Future will reflect the reality of God, who's not old and wearing out like some of us, but endlessly, laughingly new, calling us to follow him in trust into the great future that awaits us.

[Originally used at St Patrick's Cathedral, Armagh, 17th March 1994.]

Wrestling with the Angel

THERE are very few analogues to preaching but I suppose the closest is poetry, and in the case of both preaching and poetry the 'how to' questions are the easiest to answer. Organisation and method, how to start, reach the middle and how to end are all important questions, and we must think about them and develop techniques to accomplish them. But they are essentially questions about *form,* and preaching comes from the content that is poured into the form, the hot steel that's poured into the mould. The essential question about preaching is not the 'how' question, but the 'what' question. *What* is preaching? On the answer will depend the whole nature and scope of our ministry. If we pitch the answer high it will dominate our ministry, become a lifelong struggle, a source of joy and pain, a way of being. We will *become* preachers and that means we will develop a particular type of consciousness, be to some extent taken over; be, if you like, possessed, owned, ordered, commanded, almost haunted, sometimes hunted. If, on the other hand, we pitch the answer low, it will make preaching an unavoidable but unwelcome chore, a necessary but inconvenient concomitant of the Liturgy, say; or if we are loquacious, and many non-preachers are, it will provide us with happy opportunities for running off at the mouth, improving all occasions with an endless flow of ill-chosen chatter.

A great deal of non-preaching, or low-grade preaching goes on in the Church, and much of it is a source of enormous pain and boredom to our congregations; and some of it is spiritually damaging to its listeners, because it treats high and glowing matters, matters of burning importance and absolutely final intent, in a trivial or off-hand or inconsequential way. Bishop Hanson famously said that 'sermonettes make Christianettes',[1] whereas real preaching, when it is heard and submitted to, can move people to the very depths of their being, change whole cultures, the direction of nations and the very flow of history. Increasingly, I believe that preaching chooses or does not choose us, and maybe the Church should simply discern those who have been called and make it possible for them to do it, while silencing all the others. An interesting theological question is whether preaching is a charismatic gift or an administrative endowment of Holy Orders, in most cases unrealised, unactualised. I believe that even those who are not perhaps born preachers can, by their passion and longing, place themselves at the disposal of the Spirit to be made preachers, to be set alight, used by the Word.

What, then, is preaching? I would pitch the definition very high. It is a mode of divine revelation: it is one of the ways through which God chooses to encounter his children; and, as with revelation in general, it seems to conform itself to the principles and modalities of the Incarnation. That is to say, God chooses to express himself through a human instrumentality which both limits the revelation and is yet the necessary instrument and medium of the revelation. This is one reason why preachers feel they never get preaching quite right; it is why they are always reaching for the sermon they can never preach; waiting for something to be born in them, or to come through them and never quite making it. According to this definition, then, preaching is an extension or actualisation of the Incarnation.

I'm fond of Bernard Manning's definition of preaching as 'the manifestation of the incarnate word from the written word through the spoken word'.[2] Incidentally, this may be one reason why traditions that have a high view of preaching frequently have a lower view of the Eucharist, because they experience the real presence of Christ in the sermon and encounter him there. It may also be why traditions that have a high doctrine of the real presence in the Eucharist often have a low appreciation of his real presence in preaching. It seems to me, however, that to be truly Catholic and Evangelical we must cleave to the doctrine that Christ is manifested in word and sacrament, and probably only fully when they are married together. Now, if we accept this definition of preaching as revelation, it has profound consequences for the preacher.

William Temple wrote: '*The essential condition of effectual revelation is the coincidence of divinely controlled event and minds divinely illumined to read it aright.*' [3] For the purposes of this consideration we could amend that quotation to read, 'The essential condition of effectual preaching is the coincidence of divinely controlled event and minds divinely illumined to *receive and reproduce* it aright'. We can do little about 'the divinely controlled event', but as preachers it is our task to dispose ourselves to be open to its possibility so that our minds may be 'divinely illumined to read it aright', and then find the words or allow ourselves to be found by the words that will disclose it to others.

What does that disposition involve? What are the consequences of offering ourselves as human conduits of revelation? First of all, it will, to some extent, marginalise us, put us off to one side, because it will require much of our time and energy. As I have already said, the real analogues of preaching are poetry, or music, or art. All are revelatory activities and all require a discipline and an intensity that marginalise their practitioners, because they are time-consuming. Preaching takes time, because divine illumination, like artistic inspiration, is not something we can turn on like the desk lamp in our studies on Saturday nights, or Fridays if we are conscientious. It requires the development of a particular kind of consciousness, a readiness, an alertness for revelation, for in-filling, for in-flooding. It requires time for contemplation, time for reverie, solitude. If we cannot be alone, we cannot be preachers, because God speaks to us most often in solitude. I'm not actually talking about prayer, though that is clearly a part of it; I'm really talking about a kind of holy thinking, musing, listening: '*reverie*' is the best word, I think.

One ought never to generalise, of course, and some people have large resources of energy enabling them to straddle a number of vocational disciplines, but for most of us choices involve corresponding rejections and preaching demands sacrifices. We are talking about intensity and commitment here, and it may be instructive to use a non-preaching analogy. For instance, we can readily believe that a politician, say, could be a poet in the sense of dabbling in poetry, or versifying from time to time; but it is inconceivable that a poet could be a politician, because the status of poethood requires a commitment and intensity that would make the practice of politics impossible. It may be, of course, that if we believe in minimalist government we would want our poets to be politicians, but the point I'm trying to make is that the intensity and commitment required for poetry precludes many other activities, and I think the same is true of preaching. Serious preaching requires intensity and commitment of a sort that excludes, if you like, ecclesiastical politics and a certain level of commitment to administration or Church business. In other words, preachers put preaching *first,* and it is a jealous mistress that modifies all other commitments and practices. The more Protestant churches have understood this better than the rest of us; they have recognised that preaching is the primary task of the ordained ministry and have organised their system accordingly. We see less of this arrangement now, though in the Church of Scotland the minister is still expected to spend a fair bit of the week on the sermon for Sunday morning. In one or two large Protestant churches in the USA, such as Riverside Church in New York City, the senior minister is the Preaching Minister and is expected to spend a large part of the week preparing the Sunday sermon and a large part of the long summer vacation he is allowed in planning and researching the winter's preaching.

We are unlikely to achieve that privileged leisure, so one of the things we must learn to do, first of all, is to mark out some sense of priorities in our life. One way of assessing your commitment to preaching is to audit a week and discover how much time you gave to that reverie, that waiting for revelation, that cultivation of the mood that precedes the emergence of the sermon. I know that inescapable duties are imposed upon us, but a commitment of time is important and sometimes bargains can be driven with God. When I was a busy parish priest I entered into a covenant with God on the subject. I felt called to be a preacher, but I was clearly called to be many other things as well, and I made a deal with God that I would give him Friday evenings from six o'clock onwards, if he would give me what he wanted me to say. On most occasions he came through by midnight, but there were times when it was much later than that, though he always seemed to keep his side of the bargain.

The second consequence of the commitment to the preaching vocation is that it will involve us in a lifetime engagement with other revelatory sources. Revelation is the name we give to the impact of God upon human consciousness and the records of that impact. These records can still become points of revelation to us if we come to them right. T S Eliot said in *Four Quartets*: 'We had the experience but missed the meaning; but approach to the meaning restored the experience.' [4] We could also say 'that returning to the record of the experience can expand the meaning'. We must remember Bernard Manning's definition of preaching as *'the manifestation of the incarnate word from the written word through the spoken word'*. We have to learn to wait on scripture to disclose itself. Critical study need not be, but often seems to be an enemy of this process. It has often been remarked that clergy, trained in the latest critical approaches to scripture, often revert to a kind of implicit fundamentalism in the pulpit. This is a complex phenomenon but it seems to illustrate two truths about the revelatory process. We have to remember that only God is God and the vehicles of revelation, including scripture, transmit the divine but are not themselves divine; God comes through them but is not contained or limited by them. What we get is God on the slant, God's glory suddenly reflected off something that is not God but catches the majesty of his passing. This is enough excitement for seven lifetimes but there is a kind of insecure greediness in us that leads to an idolatrising dynamic whereby we divinise the instrument that conveyed the experience of God, we sanctify the mirrors that reflect his glory. The real danger that confronts humanity has never been atheism; it has always been idolatry, worshipping as God the things God has made. And the things that have been closest to God are the most dangerous. That's why religion and its forms and traditions can become divine substitutes, obstacles to real experience of God, idols. That is why the apophatic tradition of Eastern Orthodoxy is so important to us as a corrective to the excessively kataphatic tradition of the West.

A more positive way to come at the same point is to emphasise the liberatingly provisional nature of everything. Only God is God; everything else is provisional. This is a lesson the Taize Community taught me. A few years ago I was invited by the Community to visit them. I looked forward to the visit for a number of reasons, but the main one was the Taize Office Book. On and off in my ministry I had used the Taize Office and had loved its richness and elaborate use of all the best monastic precedents. I went to Evening Prayer my first night at Taize with great expectation. What I experienced was powerful and moving, but not what I expected. A psalm, a scripture lesson, a few Taize chants and a long period of silence.

'What,' I asked them afterwards, 'happened to the famous Taize Office Book?'

'We still have it,' they explained, 'and use it when appropriate, but some years ago God started sending us all these young people, for whom it was not appropriate, so we scrapped it. Everything is Provisional, you know.'

In fact, the doctrine of the Provisional is an important Taize discovery. Only God is God, everything else is Provisional, including our language about God and including our traditions of scriptural interpretation. It is an idolatrising of scripture and its interpretation that makes so many preachers reluctant to bring their minds as well as their hearts to the contemplation of scripture. God's sovereignty is not bound by our theories, but nor are our theories sovereign.

We have to learn to be humble and unanxious before scripture. One of the great preaching traditions is expository preaching of scripture, using it not as a textual corpse to be dissected, but as living oracles that still disclose the mind of God. This calls for a generous, expectant but not craven attitude to scripture. Scripture is not the enemy, but nor is it a sort of 'user's guide to salvation'. It is a mystery we can enter and find God.

But scripture is not the only source of revelation, although it will be our primary source. There are other sources of revelation and we must become acquainted with them, such as poetry, good fiction and what I call 'modern wisdom literature', letters, biographies, journals, books of epigrams. We have to learn to do two things: we have to learn to muse, to go off at a tangent, follow a trail and take notes on our musings, our trail-blazing. It is useful for this purpose to carry a notebook and pencil, and important to keep some kind of filing system, either by the old fashioned method of the commonplace book, or its modern equivalent with some kind of data base. Anything can feed our preaching because creation itself is a revelational network and all of human culture is instinct with the divine. But the secret is to enjoy poetry, art, films for their own sake, not to provide illustrations for sermons; to use them simply as sermon fodder is a kind of homiletical prostitution. If we come to human culture to enjoy it for its own sake it will yield gifts to us, moments of disclosure, annunciations of the sort Louis MacNeice talks about in his poem 'Mutations':

If there has been no spiritual change of kind
Within our species since Cro-Magnon man,
And none is looked for now, while the millennia cool,
Yet each of us has known mutations of the mind,
When the world jumped, and what had been a plan
Dissolved, and rivers ran from what had been a pool.

For every static world that you or I impose
Upon the real one must crack at times, and new
Patterns from new disorders open like a rose,
And old assumptions yield to new sensation
The stranger in the wings is waiting for his cue
The fuse is always laid to some annunciation.

Surprises keep us living: as when the first light
Surprised our infant eyes, or as when, very small
Clutching our parents' hands we toddled down a road
Where all was blank and windless both to touch and sight
Had we not suddenly raised our eyes, which showed
The long grass growing wild on top of the high wall.

For it is true, surprises break and make
As when the baton falls, and all together the hands
On the fiddle bows are pistons, or when, crouched above
His books the scholar suddenly understands
What he has thought for years – or when the inveterate rake
Finds for once that his lust is becoming love.[5]

Thirdly, commitment to preaching will involve us in the mastering of a craft or technique, even if we learn to go beyond it. We must learn the rules before we can break or transcend them. Remember the definition, 'the manifestation of the incarnate word from the written word through the spoken word'. We have to learn to love and understand words, be used by them, take risks with them, as the divine Word himself did. Preachers have to have a particular kind of courage; they have to experiment, learn a certain abandonment of the self or of self-consciousness, they have to open themselves to the extraordinary energy and confusion of words and language. And this abandonment may be embarrassing to members of their family. I know that my wife has frequently wanted to disappear through the floor as she has felt in her shyness that I have really gone over the top this time. Words are things we must learn to love and learn to respect and honour; but we must also learn to use them with daring and imagination.

Now let me turn to a fairly fundamental question that may sound purely technical and related to form, but I believe it has its own theological significance. If we have decided to be preachers, we probably have to decide whether we are to be 'manuscript preachers' or 'extempore preachers'; whether we are going to write our sermons out in full, or preach them from memory or a few notes. Each method has its advantages and disadvantages, its entirely appropriate theological justification, and it's something that only the individual can decide upon and much will depend upon the nature of the individual. As a life-long practitioner of manuscript preaching, who has only in recent years discovered the power and liberty of extempore preaching, I must admit to a certain bias in favour of manuscript preaching, and I would suggest that a lifetime of writing sermons ought to enable us to preach extempore when we need to, but the opposite is not necessarily the case. The differences are probably to do with temperament and psychology, and it's worth remembering that some of the greatest preachers have been manuscript preachers and some have preached extempore. But let me say something about the advantages and disadvantages of each method.

The advantages of manuscript preaching:

Well-prepared texts avoid unnecessary repetition, although some repetition is necessary as the story of the old preacher reminds us, when asked what the secret of his success was: 'Well, I tell them what I'm going to tell them; then I tell them; then I tell them what I've told them.' Of course, not all extempore preachers fall into the vice of repetitiousness, but I know that *I* do when I do not use a manuscript.

Manuscript preaching makes us really think out and know what we intend to say; and this does not have to be a cold and calculating thing, but it does have to be a *prepared* thing.

Manuscript preaching disciplines us to the creation of connected narratives and it helps us to be skilled wordsmiths, and this skill can be applied in all sorts of other directions, from writing parish newsletters right up to full length books.

The disadvantages are equally obvious:

There can be a deadness, a stiffness in delivery of the material so carefully prepared. We all know preachers who have been quite unjustly accused of insincerity because they have 'read' their text in an obvious and uncaptivating way. This is a genuine danger for the manuscript preacher who has not developed the technique of preaching *from* rather than simply reading *out of* the text. So manuscript preachers have to pay particular attention to delivery, and sometimes this is aided by having some dispassionate technician video a sermon being preached, without forewarning.

There can be a lack of affectivity or surprise in the manuscript preacher. If the preachers know exactly what they are going to say, how can they communicate something of the surprise, something of the joy and sorrow of the Gospel? The answer, I believe, lies in the passion with which the sermon is prepared. I have frequently, in preparing sermons, been moved to tears, not by what *I* have written, but by, as it were, what is being said through me; and this same proper affectivity can be brought, indeed *must* be brought, to the proclaiming of the sermon.

Manuscript preaching exposes us to the rather superficial accusation that we do not trust the Holy Spirit to give us a word. Well, all true preaching is done under the inspiration of the Holy Spirit and we mustn't fall into some kind of temporal fallacy that believes the Holy Spirit only inspires at 11.15 on a Sunday morning in a kind of flash-flood. This is a very primitive and superstitious notion of the Holy Spirit. It is undoubtedly true that in the midst of delivering a sermon inspiration can come and new directions and illustrations present themselves, but it's also true that the Holy Spirit is a God of order, as well as a God of freedom, surprise and play, and careful preparation does not exclude, indeed, relies upon, the prompting of the Holy Spirit. We know how easy it is to fabricate apparently extempore preaching, such as memorising a text the way an actor memorises a soliloquy. Well, there may be a certain immediacy in that, but it's no more sincere than an honest to God reliance upon a lovingly prepared text.

The advantages of extempore preaching:

The main and obvious one is its directness and its energy. As someone who practises both methods, there are times when I have known that I had to abandon a script or not be bound in any sense by it, either because of the size or age or make-up of the group, or even because of the architecture of the building.

And related to this is the importance of eye contact in preaching. This, of course, is not necessarily precluded by manuscript preaching, and, indeed, we should be careful to achieve it, no matter what our method is, but it is much easier if we are not in any sense bound to a piece of paper in front of us.

And extempore preaching is ideal in small groups, especially if we are having to sit to deliver the Word.

The disadvantages of extempore preaching:

The disadvantages are equally obvious, especially in unskilled practitioners. The most obvious is woolliness, a lack of astringency, leanness or clarity.

There is the repetitiousness I have already talked about.

Sometimes length is a problem: extempore preachers do not always know when to stop, unless, as I say, they are skilled in the art and know exactly where they are going and how to conclude.

For the lazy, the fourth disadvantage tends to be an 'unthought out' structure. If this is a weakness in the preacher it will be exaggerated by extempore preaching, whereas a manuscript, at the least, might limit the damage and reassure the hapless congregation that it will end sometime.

* * *

It's worth knowing what your bent is and following it, but it's also worth experimenting in the other technique. Manuscript preachers should, from time to time, practise extempore preaching and extempore preachers should, from time to time, submit themselves to the discipline of the crafting of a complete sermon. Many a preacher has learned how to write through the discipline of crafting sermons, though many a manuscript preacher has felt chained and bound and made heavy by commitment to the text. Let me close this exposition with a few more practical points:

First of all, we should know what our end or point or purpose in preaching is. Sometimes this can be achieved by a form of self-interrogation: what am I trying to say here? what point am I seeking to make? what conclusion am I reaching for? what is the practical outcome, consequence or direction of what I am saying?

It is important, secondly, especially in a jaded and bored culture with a narrow attention span and a low boredom threshold, to arrest and retain attention; and so some care must be given to the opening of the sermon, even though we ought to avoid the meretricious gimmick or cheap attention-getting device. Even so, there is a genuinely incarnational principle at stake here, and our Lord used it in his favourite method of discourse which was the parable. Parable in Greek is *parabola,* or *lasso,* a way of capturing attention by dragging the meaning out of a common or dramatic situation and roping it into our use. The beginning and the end of a sermon are the most important parts, but unless you grab your hearers at the beginning you are not likely to have them with you at the end. I think of the beginning of sermons as the opening arrest and spend considerable thought on how to achieve it. Woodbine Willie sometimes got the attention of his congregation by swearing at them. Telling stories is a time-tested method, but it can be tedious and clerical humour can be profoundly embarrassing, as Alan Bennett's classic sermon so aptly illustrates. It is true, of course, that certain schools of austere preachers elevate dullness to a theological principle: preaching is not entertainment, after all. Yes, but there is no reason why it can't be entertaining and our Lord's example hallows the importance of attention getting, of grabbing people where they are by some means in order to lead them on to another place.

And, thirdly, we must be honest in our exposition of the passage, allowing it to state itself, and not using it as a peg on which to hang some preconceived idea, or on which to hang some favourite topic or pre-occupation. Impatience and anxiety are the preacher's greatest enemy. They are caused by the spiritually fatal principle of self-reliance, the pressure to find a meaning in or something to say about this passage of scripture that sits stubbornly inert in front of us. We have to learn to wait expectantly for scripture to act upon us, disclose its meaning, because it is living and active. We won't hear it if we are busy bombarding it with our own questions. Preachers have to be patient, good at waiting, content to watch.

And we must learn to know ourselves so that we avoid preaching *only ourselves:* we must not use the pulpit as a vehicle for our own egotism or opinions. And we must not scold or get at people. Though God may use us prophetically, the mark of a prophet is always reluctance to castigate. No person has put it better than Reinhold Niebuhr, himself a prophet:

*Whenever a prophet is born, either inside or outside of the church,
he faces the problem of preaching repentance without bitterness
and of criticising without spiritual pride ....*

*Think of sitting Sunday after Sunday under some professional
holy man who is constantly asserting his egotism by criticising
yours. I would rebel if I were a layman. A spiritual leader who has
too many illusions is useless. One who has lost his illusions about
mankind and retains his illusions about himself is insufferable.
Let the process of disillusionment continue until the self is included.
At that point, of course, only religion can save from the enervation
of despair. But it is at that point that true religion is born.*[6]

Remember what Goethe said: 'We must beware of those in
whom the desire to punish is strong.'[7] We must suspect ourselves
when we are too eager to attack, injure or express our own anger.

It has to be admitted that bishops lead an odd sort of life. They
spend a lot of time preaching at special occasions and this removes
them from the main challenge facing the preacher, the need to
maintain an appropriate level of quality and significance over a
long period. Preachers in the parish context, which is where most of
them operate, have to learn to pace themselves like long-distance
runners. Preaching is not a series of short sprints; it's more like a
campaign than a single sports meeting or battle. Preachers are there
to form or build up the spiritual lives of their people, so they must
plan for the long haul with courses, preaching from whole books of
the Bible, such as series on the Epistles, the different theological
emphases of the Gospel writers and so on, as well as on doctrinal
and devotional themes, such as the formation of Christian teaching
on, say, the meaning of the death of Christ or the Christian understanding of God's nature. Much preaching is unhelpfully moralistic,
exhorting people from the pulpit to toe the Christian line on highly
complex issues, always assuming there is a single 'Christian' line.
Much of this is unhelpful, but preachers cannot eschew the moral
dimension of Christianity, though it is often as much about inviting
people to understand as to judge. There is an old and useful dis-

tinction between preaching and teaching, between the proclamation of the Gospel, good news as distinguished from good advice, and teaching, a more objective, maybe less challenging offering of an account of what Christians believe and how they come to believe it. 'Preaching for a verdict,' proclaiming the good news of God in a way that will challenge and convert people, is taxing and we cannot expect to achieve it all of the time. Parish preaching, anyway, presupposes the existence of an already converted congregation, so that pastoral preaching will concern itself with deepening and informing the Christian life of the people of God. Nevertheless, preaching, the disposing of ourselves to be used as God's revelatory vehicle, is the true vocation of the preacher and if we offer ourselves for this work God will use us, sometimes when we least expect it.

[Originally used at the Festival of Preaching, York, September 1992.]

1   In an article in *The Times*.
2   Source unknown.
3   Source unknown.
4   T S Eliot: 'Four Quartets' from *East Coker*.
5   Louis MacNeice: *Collected Poems* (London: Faber & Faber).
6   Reinhold Niebuhr: *Leaves from the Notebook of a Tamed Cynic*.
7   Source unknown.

The Use of the Bible

SOMETIME during the 1970s a television series was made about Winston Churchill. It covered the period of the 1930s and it was called 'Churchill: The Years in the Wilderness', or something like that. An extra-terrestrial viewer of the series with only a surface knowledge of English would have been puzzled by the title. Churchill was shown at his London home or painting on canvasses and building brick walls at his country home at Chartwell in Kent. He was shown in the House of Commons and at meetings in London's Clubland, his cigar in his right hand and a large glass of brandy frequently in the left. It was a world of heavy opulence, sombre, filled with black Daimlers, leather upholstery and powerful men. Our hypothetical viewer from Outer Space would wait in vain for shots of the hero trudging across trackless wastes or hacking his way through thick bush. We know, of course, that the wilderness of the title was a piece of cultural telegraphy or shorthand, packed with meaning and association, a good example of the way language carries a people's tradition and experience folded concisely into metaphors and symbols that have to be interpreted and decoded for the stranger.

– 'Judas,' he hissed, and we know exactly what he means.
– 'The man's an absolute Philistine,' he drawled, and we understand.
– 'She's a real Jezebel,' and we get the message.

The Bible is the source of all these stereotypes and many more, but the Bible is much more than a compendium of stock characters, a sort of central casting unit for the human drama. It provides us with every conceivable type of human nature: the traitor, the hero, the flawed leader, the lonely prophet whose voice cries in the wilderness, the strong woman married to a contemptible husband, the impulsive braggart, the quiet faithful man, the searcher, the persecutor, the madman, the beggar, the thief. All life is there and every way of being human, and it is the Bible that has given us many of our reference points for mapping human nature. But the Bible does more than this. It provides us not only with examples of the stock characters of the human drama, but also with all the enduring themes in the human story; it confronts us with the permanent elements in the human condition, the great inescapable realities of life. And it does this in a way that is useful to us as we explore the human condition, seek to understand our own life, search for personal meaning. I deliberately used an undramatic little word there: I said that the Bible is *useful* to us, it can be *used.* And I mean a particular kind of use. Of course, it can be used in many ways: it can be read as literature, for example, and a knowledge of it is still useful if you do crossword puzzles; it provides theological students in pursuit of higher degrees with inexhaustible possibilities for research. But these are not the kind of uses I had in mind. That way of using the Bible sees it as a quarry of inert material which we can exploit for our own purposes. There is a more ancient use of Scripture than that, and when it is discovered the Bible comes alive in our hands, like a sharp, two-edged sword that probes and questions *us.* If we will enter its world, the Bible will introduce us to the landscape of our own soul. This is part of what we mean when we say the Bible has authority. It has the power, when meditated on, to interpret the meaning of our existence to us and bring us up against the mystery we call God.

Behind the title of that series of programmes on Winston Churchill there lies one of the great biblical themes, the wilderness theme. Churchill spent the thirties in the political wilderness and in something of a personal wilderness, too. The biblical echo behind that way of describing Churchill's experience was, of course, the long period during which the children of Israel wandered in the wilderness before making it to the promised land of milk and honey, the land of Canaan. They had made their escape from Egypt, but it was a long time before they were able to settle in another country. That is one of the more straightforward ways to describe the wilderness theme in the Bible. There are others, but biographers of the great like their heroes to spend some time in the wilderness, whence they are called to fame or the doing of some great work. The call finally came to Churchill to come out of the wilderness, and he had his finest hour.

That is a fairly straightforward use of a biblical metaphor; it is a literary device, a convenient way to summarise the tone and essence of a particular time, a biographer's whim, something formal and external. I do not know what inner resources Churchill turned to during his wilderness years, apart from his own sense of destiny, but the painting and the wall-building suggest that, like most people at some time in their lives, he sought consolation and distraction from personal emptiness by various time-filling devices, as well as the unavoidable obligation to earn his living. But it is at least conceivable that Churchill might have sought an understanding of his situation and a way of interpreting it by meditating on Scripture. Adversity has many uses but, as with life itself, we can be so busy filling it with activity that we never confront the thing as it is in itself. Scripture offers us a series of symbolic events or stories that connect with and make sense of our own private story. All the events that are used in this way began as real history, though the historical core in the story as we now have it is usually obscure and to a very great extent unrecoverable. But something important has happened to these stories that has lifted them from time past into a dramatic present that makes them usable by us, as they have been used before us and will continue to be used after us. It is hard to describe what has happened to these stories or how they can be used, in the abstract. Some things, most of the important and quirky things in life, cannot be translated, there are no apt or perfect verbal equivalents for them. The moment when you first find your balance and are actually riding a bike is one of these moments. So is swimming for the first time or making love or hang-gliding. The experience comes only with the experience. Their meaning is found only *within* and never outside the experience.

Anyway, these events, remote in themselves, have been so meditated upon and wondered at and interpreted, that they have been released into time and are usable by us, very much the way a communications satellite, separated from the rocket that got it there, is available to the whole world. One of the main uses of Scripture in its universal availability is its private use in meditation and self-discovery. Scripture has always played an important role in private devotion, and church libraries of a certain generation are full of little books helping us to meditate on Scripture, to milk its meaning and apply it to our own situation. I was brought up on just such a tradition and I recall a certain book of meditations that all students at Kelham were given. It provided a meditation for every day of the year based on the lessons at the daily Eucharist. I also think of Father Andrew of the Society of the Divine Compassion, who wrote a very influential book of meditations on the Church's year. And I think now of the new interest in Ignatian Spirituality, which uses Scripture as a means of personal challenge and discovery and encounter with God's will for our lives. Gerald Hughes' book, *God of Surprises*, adapts and applies the Ignatian method for using Scripture in a refreshingly modern way. As a matter of purely personal interest, I used the book during my retreat before I was consecrated Bishop, and I remember still a meditation I did on the Gadarene Demoniac guided by Father Hughes' book. One would not expect the Gadarene Demoniac to be a very fruitful topic for private meditation but it was profoundly helpful, because it enabled me to encounter certain forces and repressed elements of my own personality which I was reluctant to acknowledge.

So the private use of Scripture is important, but it is not the primary use. Scripture is above all the record of a people's encounter with God in history and it is the corporate use of Scripture that is primary. This is primarily experienced in worship but it can also be experienced in small group study, or even in the use of Scripture as a way of interpreting and meditating upon our political situation. This is certainly how the Black community in America has used Scripture in its worship and in its corporate meditation upon its own place in American history. I can remember visiting Black churches in East Harlem in the sixties during the Civil Rights Movement, when the story of the Exodus became the living symbol of the Black experience. Martin Luther King's rhetoric was laced with biblical imagery as he tried to lead his people from slavery in Egypt to the promised land of freedom and equality in American society. If you went to worship in a Black church you found these great biblical themes burningly alive. They were not matters of purely archeological or historical interest; they were burningly and vividly contemporary. To hear these great Scripture passages from the Old and new Testaments in a Black church punctuated with the great spirituals that they sang, such as 'Come out the wilderness' and 'Go down, Moses', was to experience the Black community's great longing for liberation. Used like this, Scripture becomes a living interpreter and way of embodying the history of a people. It is thus that Desmond Tutu used Scripture during the long struggle against apartheid in South Africa; and in the base communities in South America, where poor Christians struggle against oppression, it is Scripture that helps them not only interpret their condition but engage in the struggle for freedom and more abundant living. Scripture is not a sort of archeological site filled with dead relics and reminders of the past. When used in this way, as the Letter to the Hebrews reminds us, it is alive and active and sharper than a two-edged sword.

Our use of Scripture in worship may be less dramatic than that, but the principles are the same. Our method of using Scripture in worship is one which is based upon the same premise: hearing the great record of God's action in history and its impact on the souls of men and women rehearsed over and over again. In this way, we internalise it and make it part of our own experience.

This is especially true in Anglican worship, because we have understood the Resurrection Gospel as something that is present to the experience of believers in every generation, and by means of the ordered reading of Scripture the community of baptised Christians participates over and over again in the redemption won by Christ. This points to the importance of adequate lectionaries, methods whereby the story of our redemption in Scripture is laid before us in a systematic way over the months and years. Most good modern lectionaries are based on a three year cycle of readings, in which the story of our creation and redemption is rehearsed over and over again, so that it becomes integrated with our own experience both as Church and as individual soul. This use of Scripture in worship is based on what we might call a *sacramental* view of Scripture. A sacrament is a symbol that actually conveys value and meaning to us: a pound note is a sacrament in this sense, it is not itself a pound but it conveys the value, I suppose originally, of a pound of gold, to us: it conveys the value of what it signifies. And so does Scripture. It tells the story of our creation, redemption and the work of our sanctification. The words read in the assembly of the faithful actually convey the meaning and value of the experience. They are not simply words written in ink on paper, they express the living reality of God's love and redemption.

This is seen most particularly and dramatically in Holy Week, when the whole pace of the Church's year slows down. Throughout the Christian year whole millennia can be truncated into three or four weeks, as is the case in the season of Advent when we think about the ancient human longing for true knowledge of God, looking into the clouds to behold his coming, longing for Emmanuel to be among us. In the four weeks before Christmas we listen again to those great heart-bursting passages from Isaiah in which God is exhorted to rain down mercy upon us and to send his light into our darkness. And then there's a slowing down of the film and when we get to Christmas we're at walking pace, human pace, as we follow the birth narratives up to the Feast of the Epiphany.

And then things speed up again and we hear lessons that recount the public ministry of our Lord, leading us to the great narratives of the temptation during the season of Lent. Then, as I have said, the whole pace slows down and for a week we dwell minute by minute upon the story of our Lord's passion and death; we track his last week on earth from the triumphal entry into Jerusalem on Palm Sunday to his dying and rising again a week later. The Holy Week services and the long passages from Scripture that they enshrine are a vivid example of the use of Scripture in worship as a means whereby we identify with and internalise the meaning of our Lord's passion and resurrection. It is an enormous privilege to take part in these services where they are fully celebrated. The tradition is to read or sing all the Passion accounts from all the four Gospels during Holy Week, though the Matthew Passion is traditionally associated with the Palm Sunday liturgy and the Passion according to John is associated traditionally with the Good Friday liturgy. To hear these expertly sung or expertly read in choral recitation can be a draining and moving experience. Indeed, to go through the intricacies of the Liturgy in Holy Week and Easter is to experience all over again the glory and drama of that divine dying and that rising from the tomb to be with us forever.

Then we move in our liturgical worship into the great Forty Days, and again there's a kind of slowing down of the tempo as we are led from the Easter Garden through the great events of the post-Resurrection appearances right up to the Feast of Pentecost seven weeks later. 'Pentecost' means the Fiftieth Day. The name was first given to the Jewish Feast of Weeks, which fell on the fiftieth day after the Passover when the first fruits of the corn harvest were presented and the giving of the Law of Moses was commemorated. According to the Acts of the Apostles, the Holy Spirit descended on the apostles on this the fiftieth day after the Resurrection, and the same name was applied by the Church to the feast celebrating this event, popularly called Whit Sunday, that is 'White' Sunday. The 'White' is generally taken to refer to the ancient custom of the wearing of white baptismal robes by the newly baptised at the Feast of Pentecost. It ranks after Easter as the second festival in the Church and is the climax of the Christian year. After it we move into the long slow season nowadays called 'after Pentecost', but before the recent liturgical changes known as the period 'after Trinity', during which everything slows down and we hear passages from Scripture of a more general nature and we listen to the teaching of our Lord as expounded in parable and discourse, rather than focusing upon the incidents in his own life and death. I am very fond of a poem written by John Meade Falconer which captures this long slow period, which I used to find very boring as a youth, but now, as my own years speed up, I find rather consoling. It's called 'After Trinity':

We have done with dogma and divinity
　　　Easter and Whitsun past,
The long, long Sundays after Trinity
　　　Are with us at last;
The passionless Sundays after Trinity,
　　　Neither feast-day nor fast.

Christmas comes with plenty,
　　　Lent spreads out its pall,
But these are five and twenty,
　　　The longest Sundays of all;
The placid Sundays after Trinity,
　　　Wheat-harvest, fruit-harvest, Fall.

Spring with its burst is over,
　　　Summer has had its day,
The scented grasses and clover
　　　Are cut, and dried into hay;
The singing-birds are silent,
　　　And the swallows flown away.

Post pugnam pausa fiet;
　　　Lord, we have made our choice;
In the stillness of autumn quiet,
　　　We have heard the still, small voice.
We have sung Oh where shall Wisdom?
　　　Thick paper, folio, Boyce.

Let it not all be sadness,
       Not omnia vanitas,
Stir up a little gladness
       To lighten the Tibi cras;
Send us that little summer,
       That comes with Martinmas.

When still the cloudlet dapples
       The windless cobalt-blue,
And the scent of gathered apples
       Fills all the store-rooms through,
The gossamer silvers the bramble,
       The lawns are gemmed with dew.

An end of tombstone Latinity,
       Stir up sober mirth,
Twenty-fifth after Trinity,
       Kneel with the listening earth,
Behind the Advent trumpets
       They are singing Emmanuel's birth.[1]

And back we come again to the great longing of Advent and the greater joy of Christmas. Christian worship, especially in the order- ed traditions of Catholic worship, tell and re-tell, live and re-live the great mysteries of Scripture. But it is not out of nostalgia; the Christian Liturgy is not a kind of eucharistic Burns Supper in which we look back to the past. No, in Christian worship the great mysteries of the Bible are experienced now as living and active. It is *our* story that is told, it is our longing that is constantly expressed, our redemp- tion that is constantly celebrated.

The Bible is not history; it is our story.

[Originally used at Christ Church, Edinburgh, February 1989.]

1   Source unknown. Meade Falconer was a minor 20th century poet.